JESUS *the* REBEL

BEARER *of* GOD'S PEACE *and* JUSTICE

JOHN DEAR, S.J.

SHEED & WARD
FRANKLIN, WISCONSIN

As an apostolate of the Priests of the Sacred Heart,
a Catholic religious congregation, the mission of Sheed & Ward is to publish books of
contemporary impact and enduring merit in Catholic Christian thought and action. The
books published, however, reflect the opinions of their authors and are not meant to
represent the official position of the Priests of the Sacred Heart.

2000

Sheed & Ward
7373 South Lovers Lane Road
Franklin, Wisconsin 53132
1-800-266-5564

Printed in the United States of America
Cover and interior design by Madonna Gauding

LIBRARY OF CONGRESS CATALOGING-IN-PUBLICATION DATA

Dear, John, 1959—
Jesus the rebel : bearer of God's peace and justice / John Dear.
p. cm.
ISBN 1-58051-073-6 (alk. paper)
Jesus Christ—Meditations. 2. Peace—Religious aspects—Catholic
Church—Meditations. 3. Christianity and justice—Catholic Church—Meditations.
4. Nonviolence—Religious aspects—Catholic Church—Meditations. I. Title.

BT306.4 .D35 2000
232—dc21

99-056804

For Jackson,
"on the side of the rebel Jesus"

Contents

FOREWORD

Now,
there are
many other things
that Jesus did.

If
they were all
written down
one by one,

I doubt
there would be
room enough
in the entire world

to hold the books
to record them!
(see John 21:25)

The exclamation point in the above quotation is my own. It aims to record the vehement hyperbole that winds John's Gospel to a close. What a grand finale, what a flourish of the quill—and that by a hand so habitually cool, a mind so collected!

It is no news at all—John the Divine was proven right. Books concerning Jesus were already under way in his lifetime. They continued to flood the world, a very deluge of devotion, interrogation, worshipfulness, scholarship opaque and serviceable, meditation, adulation—and now and again a sting of vituperation, to be sure!

It appears that the enigmatic rabbi, his tropes and tales, his wonders and claims, the all but immeasurable heights and breadths and depths into which he reaches—into which he stretches us—that is One, at once transparent and opaque, must be dealt with again and yet again, an imperative as mysterious as it is endemic to every age and clime.

In this book, one such effort graces us—and in a nearly graceless time. It is arguable that our species, armed as we are with an arsenal of unspeakable ways and means, has never been more obsessively bent in a direction precisely contrary to Jesus' way. Our prospects, and those of our children, are more somber than a palette of dark words may convey. We are beyond doubt a murderous clan, hell-bent. Are we terminal, suicidal as well?

Whether or not, there is good reason, as John Dear insists, to open the Gospel; to put ourselves to a task both crucial and thankless—a discipline of spirit; to come to a measure of self-knowledge; to know the world for what it is—fallen; to know ourselves for who we are—fallen.

The ironies elaborated in these pages are unnerving. John Dear writes at length of our vocation. Quite simply, we are called to be disciples of Jesus. Woebegone as we are, heirs of a culture splitting at the seams as sound purpose falls to rot. Disciples—amid scoundrels, whose politics are a lethal mix of contempt and larceny, who seize the throttle of authority and speed catastrophe along in a blood blur. Amid such moral disarray, we are called to be disciples—summoned, despite ourselves, to surpass our sorry selves; to go counter; to cast sand in the killing gears; to succor as best we may, the victims.

Thus John Dear and his book. Its strengths will repay attention. His eye is on far horizons, his feet firm planted. He knows his Subject well, with the knowledge that comes from a compassionate heart, witnessing the suffering of the innocent.

As a friend of the author, I rejoice. Pondering his Jesus, I reflect that author and Subject are of a piece, one. It is this I admire and celebrate and learn from. The book ventures into no act, no parable, no inference of the gospel that John has not decoded, tried on for size, risked his good name in witness to. Again and again, John Dear has walked where holy words lead: to a high mountain of instruction, into the desert of forty days, into the garden of anguish. He has poured his blood on nuclear weaponry and has paid up in kangaroo courts and unspeakable jails. He has trekked about the world bearing the gospel in hand and heart, a wing-shod messenger of peace. He has lived in solidarity with the wretched of the earth—whose plight, as he well knows, is the mean feat of abominable economics and killer instincts on rampage. In this century, in this land, cleft in fragments of gigantic disorder, what a witness!

I can scarce credit my good fortune. For many a hard year now, this good and immensely talented man of God has graced my life with his friendship. Through him, I find it less improbable that I can live decently in a ferocious world, less likely that I cave in to the cultural lot, a witch's brew of functional despair and half a life.

I have a vignette to close this. As John prepared his first Mass in a poor church in Washington, he asked me to say a few words. I did so, in these terms: A year previous, I had said to a friend, "The Jesuits don't deserve John Dear." And the friend retorted, "But you do."

She was wrong—and in a sense, she was right as well. John's friendship is of such moment, so lifts the heart, as to raise me to a species of deserving. Thank you, John. In you, Jesus is believable.

Daniel Berrigan, S.J.

INTRODUCTION

F lannery O'Connor describes Jesus as "that ragged figure flitting from tree to tree in the back of the mind." He haunts us, sneaks up on us, pursues us, like an agent after the FBI's most wanted. Eventually, he corners us. But when we turn to face him, nothing's there. He vanishes from sight—and the game of life begins again.

The following pages reflect on the mysterious comings and goings of Jesus according to various gospel episodes. Jesus was anything but passive, complacent, or corrupt. Rather, he was the beloved of God on fire with love for every human being who ever lived. As such, he was trouble from day one: trouble for the establishment, trouble for the religious elite, trouble for the rulers, trouble for the war-making empire.

Jesus was a rebel—but with a difference. He was the revolutionary face of the God of nonviolence. In a world of total violence given over to death, the incarnation of the God of Life can only mean trouble for the status quo—the empire of death.

These gospel stories console and energize me; they also humble and disturb me. As the Word of God, they stand in judgment upon our culture, our world, ourselves.

Yet, when we listen closely, we hear not judgment but compassion. We hear a word of love calling us to the fullness of life. We hear the good news of peace and hope.

In these gospel times, that ragged revolutionary figure continues to stalk us, refusing to give up on us, hoping to catch us off guard. With shock and surprise, we turn around, expecting to see him. But, again, he disappears behind some tree in the back of our mind—and the mystery of life continues. Perhaps we are slowly and finally learning that he wants each of us to carry on his journey of revolutionary nonviolence.

It is this mysterious, playful, hide-and-seek God who makes life interesting, meaningful, hopeful, even joyful. May these pages lure him out again, that he might find us—ready and waiting and willing, this time, to take up his work of peace and justice.

John Dear, S.J.

chapter one

THE BELOVED

After all the people had been baptized and Jesus also had been baptized and was praying, heaven was opened and the holy Spirit descended upon him in bodily form like a dove. And a voice came from heaven, "You are my beloved Son; with you I am well pleased." (Luke 3:21–22)

It happened to Thomas Merton on the Long Island Railroad. It was February 1937, and Merton—a wisecracking Columbia graduate student who prided himself on his cynicism and lack of faith—had spent the day in the city. While window-shopping along Manhattan's Fifth Avenue he noticed Etienne Gilson's *The Spirit of Medieval Philosophy* on display in the window of Scribner's bookstore. Because he enjoyed studying French medieval literature, he went in and purchased the book. Later, on the train ride home to Douglaston, Long Island, where he was staying at the time, Merton opened the book and saw the *Nihil Obstat,* the imprimatur of the local bishop. He had been conned!

Because religious censorship nauseated him, Merton swore that he wouldn't touch the book again. "The feeling of disgust and deception struck me like a knife in the pit of the stomach," he wrote in his best-selling autobiography, *The Seven Storey Mountain.* He instinctively thought to throw the book out the window "at the houses of Woodside—to get rid of it as something dangerous and unclean."

But Merton's curiosity was piqued; he did not pitch the book out the window. Rather, he read a page, then another—and by the end of the day, he accepted every word of it as truth. "God is the pure act of being," Gilson explained. "Of course," Merton thought.

A few months later, while sitting in his room at Columbia University reading the life of the Jesuit poet Gerard Manley Hopkins, Merton put the book down, went outdoors in the rain, and walked nine blocks to Corpus Christi Church. There he told the priest that he wanted to be baptized. He had become a believer.

Ten years earlier, avowed atheist Dorothy Day was living with radical activist Foster Batterham in a small colony of Communists along the Staten Island beach. Exhausted from years of demonstrations, broken relationships, and endless wandering, Day enjoyed quiet days and long walks on the beach. For the first time in her life, she felt happy. This new, contemplative peace led her to pray and, as she walked alone along the beach, she gave thanks for the beauty of creation and the wonder of life itself. With time, Day found herself unwittingly turning to the God of Life. Later, when she became pregnant, she knew the time had come to embrace the life of faith. She would raise her child in the Church.

When her daughter, Tamar, was born, Day was baptized alongside her child and dedicated her life to the gospel of Jesus. Her common-law husband, Foster, refused to accept such folly, however, and left her. For the next few years, Day prayed and wrote and searched for a way to serve others, especially those who were poor and marginalized. Then one day Peter Maurin showed up at her door, and the *Catholic Worker* was born.

Although I am not in the same ballpark as these major league Christians, something happened to me, too. Years of searching reached a climax while I was a college student at Duke University in Durham, North Carolina. A wild fraternity member, I left the Church and dreamed of becoming a lawyer, a newspaper publisher like my father or, better yet, a rock star. When a bout of bronchitis following my sophomore year left me resting at home during the summer to read and reflect on the meaning of life, I returned to campus in the fall of my junior year and volunteered to serve prisoners at a state psychiatric hospital. The contrast between their poverty and powerlessness and my family's and fraternity's wealth and power turned me upside-down. I began to question my career ambitions, my values, and the meaning of my life. I was plunged into a dark night of the soul—a search for purpose and spiritual fulfillment.

If God did not exist, I reasoned, then why not turn my back on these helpless inmates, make as much money as I can, and run wild all my life?

Indeed, why not be violent, selfish, and greedy? If, on the other hand, God does exist, then how could I waste another precious minute pursuing big bucks, neglecting the poor, and seeking selfish comforts? If God is real and alive, I thought, then life has meaning, the universe is on the side of justice for the poor, and I better wake up.

I began to pray and started reading the Gospels. As the second semester of my junior year began, I enrolled in a course called "The History of Christianity in North America." One February afternoon, while sitting alone in my fraternity dorm room reading the life of Elizabeth Ann Seton for a term paper, I came to my senses. Of course I believe in God! Of course life has purpose! Of course humanity is called to love and serve one another in the light of God's grace! Christ is present all around me, in everyone I meet, especially in those who are poor and disenfranchised. Suddenly, in a moment of spontaneous grace, I recognized a deep desire to give my life completely to Jesus, to spend my days serving Christ in the poor, to proclaim God's reign of peace and love, and to be ordained, one day, a priest in the Society of Jesus.

As sunlight poured into the room that winter afternoon, my dark night of despair lifted and the light of consolation filled my soul. I dropped my book and ran across campus to the university chapel, a towering Gothic cathedral. I walked down the center aisle and cornered Father Joe Burke, the chaplain—and a Jesuit—who was preparing a special prayer service of repentance and penance.

"I want to give my life to God," I announced. "And I want to become a Jesuit priest."

"Well, let's talk about it," he said smiling and chuckling.

And so we did. It was Ash Wednesday, 1980.

Life, I'm learning, is a long journey toward God. If we enter that journey with all our hearts, we will experience a breakthrough somewhere along the way. We will recognize the presence of God in our lives, our history, our world—and we will never be the same. Indeed, we will realize that we are loved unconditionally by God and called to love and serve God present in all other human beings. This breakthrough, traditionally marked by the early Christians with baptism, often begins a deeper searching and a series of breakthroughs. But it is a watershed moment when we know to the depths of our souls that we are loved by a loving God who is drawing us into God's own loving heart.

This breakthrough is, indeed, momentous because we break through the claims of the culture around us. Every day the culture tries to name us, insisting that we are nothing, non-human. It labels us as outsiders, trouble-makers, or enemies. Or worse, it ignores us altogether. But in Jesus we hear an entirely different, infinitely more consoling, life-giving word. Indeed, we hear through Jesus, "You are not a nobody; you are my beloved!"

From that moment on, like Jesus, we know ourselves as the beloved son of God, the beloved daughter of God. We no longer identify ourselves merely as a parent or a child, a teacher or a businessperson, a man or a woman, a North American or an African or a European. Rather, we understand ourselves as the beloved of God and, knowing this identity, we want to remain faithful to our true selves. We begin to realize that the revolution of the world begins not out there somewhere but within ourselves—where we live faithful to God's vision and understanding of who we are.

According to the synoptic Gospels, Jesus, too, experiences a breakthrough. He has a spiritual experience by the Jordan River that propels him to the desert, to his public ministry in Galilee and, finally, to his death in Jerusalem. Like other seekers, Jesus goes to the Jordan River to be baptized by the great prophet, John. As he wades into the river and is dunked under water by the prophet, he is told to repent.

After his baptism, Jesus prays and, while at prayer, the contemplative Jesus experiences God's presence. As the Spirit of God comes upon him in bodily form, like a dove, Jesus hears God say, "You are my beloved Son; with you I am well pleased." These consoling words transform Jesus, speak of God's affirmation and confirmation, encourage Jesus in his life of intimate fidelity to God, and set him on fire in the Spirit of God. Most of all, these words announce to Jesus who he is. By the Jordan River, he discovers his identity. He is "the beloved of God." For the rest of his life he will understand himself and his mission in the light of this revelation. He welcomes it, accepts it, and honors it, and remains true to it until his final breath on the cross. Herein lies the radical breakthrough, the revolution of Jesus. Not only does life make sense, not only does God exist, but God loves and affirms Jesus and, through Jesus, all humanity. Nothing will ever be the same. With the Spirit of God upon him, Jesus then walks into the desert to pray and fast, to ponder the meaning of this spiritual experience, and to prepare himself for what lies ahead.

Jesus is faithful not only to God but to himself as God's beloved. He lives his remaining days from within what Thomas Merton called his "true self." Because he knows now who he really is, God's beloved, he can go forward into the world and call people to God and to himself. He can trust God even when everything falls apart and death approaches. He lives his life in the framework of this core identity—and he challenges his followers to do the same.

This breakthrough could not have happened if Jesus was not a person of quiet intimate prayer—in other words, a listener. Jesus listens attentively for the voice of God. I imagine that he spent his youth quietly reflecting on God, studying the Scriptures, learning the rhythm of silence from his humble parents, and looking for God each day in his intimate prayer. As he grows, he keeps vigil for God's voice, cultivating silence and solitude. He becomes a true contemplative, seeking God with every deed, every word, every breath. And then one day, behold, a breakthrough.

Because Jesus keeps a quiet inner disposition—he listens—he is available when God speaks. He can hear the voice of God because he has learned to listen quietly for that inner voice in his contemplative prayer—and he takes to heart what he hears. He obeys the voice from heaven and is transformed and sent into the world.

As Jesus' baptized followers, we, too, sit in silent, intimate prayer and listen attentively for the voice of God, the voice of Jesus our beloved. At some point in our lives, as we enter the silent, contemplative prayer of listening, the Spirit of God comes upon us. We hear an inner voice call us, intimately and personally, "my beloved." On that day, like Jesus, we know who we are. We know that we can go forward in the consolation of God's love, radiating that love throughout our war-torn world.

Knowing ourselves to be the beloved of God carries immediate personal, spiritual, and social implications. As people of contemplative prayer, for example, we listen attentively, in the silence of our hearts, to the loving, consoling voice of God. We listen to that voice from heaven tell us that we are God's beloved, and we come to realize that every other human being in history is a beloved son or daughter of God as well. From now on these "others" are our beloved sisters and brothers. We love everyone and refuse to hurt or kill or remain silent in the face of human suffering and oppression. The revolution of transforming love has begun. We have entered what Henri Nouwen calls "the Life of the Beloved."

This life of unrestricted love becomes possible in that breakthrough moment because our hearts come to know that we are part of God's beloved family, the sisters and brothers of Jesus, members of the one human family. We turn enemies into friends and friends into true sisters and brothers. We eagerly anticipate life in the communion of saints by revealing and forming that communion here and now with all we meet. Indeed, life will never be the same.

After his baptism, Jesus lives every minute of his life as the beloved of God. His self-understanding involves attentive, intimate, quiet prayer; the public work of announcing God's coming reign of justice and peace; steadfast adherence to the way of nonviolence; resistance to all that denies or rejects God's nonviolent love; and trust in God until the moment of death. Most of all, his self-understanding means radical obedience to this beloved God.

As his public life becomes a string of civil disobedience actions against injustice, Jesus' inner life deepens in this radical obedience to God. He does not offer allegiance to the idols and institutions of the world, whether that be the Roman Empire or the religious elite. Rather, his allegiance is given completely to God and God's reign of justice and mercy. When it becomes clear that his revolutionary love for God and all its social implications are going to be rejected by everyone, Jesus clings even more to this beloved God, remaining faithful to the bitter end.

Throughout the accounts of Jesus' transformation by the Jordan River looms the great figure of John the Baptist, who wanders through the desert denouncing the injustice of the world, attracting great crowds, and calling people to repentance and conversion. He announces the coming "of one greater than I, one who will baptize with fire and the Holy Spirit" (see Matthew 3:11–12). He expects a revolutionary messiah sent by God who will gather his followers into guerilla military units, storm the imperial forces, defeat the empire, and reclaim Jerusalem for Israel.

Then, when he sees the Spirit of God rest on Jesus, John the Baptist knows that the Anointed One has appeared. But as he points people to Jesus and starts to "decrease," he begins to have his doubts. This Jesus isn't organizing a violent overthrow of the empire for the sake of Yahweh. "Perhaps I am wrong," John thinks. After Herod arrests him, John sends two messengers to inquire once and for all if Jesus is really the one sent from God.

Shortly before the king executes him, John gets his answer:

> "Go and tell John what you have seen and heard: the blind regain their sight, the lame walk, lepers are cleansed, the deaf hear, the dead are raised, the poor have the good news proclaimed to them. And blessed is the one who takes no offense at me" (Luke 7:22).

The Baptist dies in prison knowing that the revolution of God has come—and in much greater ways than he could ever imagine. Jesus has started a permanent revolution of transforming nonviolence. Indeed, the reign of God is breaking through here and now.

In his revolutionary life, Jesus unveils the transforming love God has for us, and we can have for God and one another. As God calls Jesus "my beloved," Jesus learns to call God "my beloved" in response. Jesus is in love with God. As his baptized followers—as brothers and sisters of "the beloved"—we, too, fall in love with God. In that falling in love with God, we gladly turn our lives around and go wherever our God leads us. In that spirit of love, claiming our belovedness, we follow Jesus anywhere on the journey of revolutionary love. Just as John the Baptist rejoiced in imagining himself as the best man to Jesus, the bridegroom, we, too, rejoice in the presence of Jesus.

Jesus knows that he has to plumb the depths within if he is to walk through the world calling people to the reign of God. Filled with the Spirit of radical love, he drops everything and walks alone into the desert. As we enter into this new life of radical discipleship with our beloved Jesus, we, too, drop everything and walk with him wherever he goes, to confront the demons within and to learn what it will mean to be faithful to God.

chapter two

THE DESERT

Jesus was led by the Spirit into the desert to be tempted by the devil. He fasted for forty days and forty nights, and afterwards he was hungry. The tempter approached and said to him, "If you are the Son of God, command that these stones become loaves of bread." He said in reply, "It is written:

> *'One does not live by bread alone,*
> > *but by every word that comes forth from the mouth of God.'"*

Then the devil took him to the holy city, and made him stand on the parapet of the temple, and said to him, "If you are the Son of God, throw yourself down. For it is written:

> *'He will command his angels concerning you'*
> > *and 'with their hands they will support you,*
> *lest you dash your foot against a stone.'"*

Jesus answered him, "Again it is written, 'You shall not put the Lord, your God, to the test.'" Then the devil took him up to a very high mountain, and showed him all the kingdoms of the world in their magnificence, and he said to him, "All these I shall give to you, if you will prostrate yourself and worship me." At this, Jesus said to him, "Get away, Satan! It is written:

> *'The Lord, your God, shall you worship*
> > *and him alone shall you serve.'"*

Then, the devil left him and, behold, angels came and ministered to him. (Matthew 4:1–11)

In the Nevada desert stands the glittering greed of Las Vegas as well as the world's greatest violence: the nuclear arsenal of the U.S. nuclear test site. For the past five decades, our government has exploded gigantic holes on the desert floor, released radiation into the air, and poisoned that beautiful land. Thousands of acres have been rendered uninhabitable.

Every year since the early 1980s, Christians have gathered in the Nevada desert during Lent for weekend retreats and prayerful civil disobedience to protest ongoing nuclear weapons testing. There, as we confront our violence in the silence of the desert, we discover the presence of God. The desert, we are learning, is a testing ground of not only our nuclear violence but also of gospel nonviolence.

After he hears God call him "my beloved," Jesus goes into the desert to find out what it means to be God's beloved. Before he can minister in Galilee and enter Jerusalem with a word of peace, he has to walk to the world's margins to discover within himself the strength to resist the temptations of violence and to cling to God. On the margin, away from the powers of the world, we, too, hear the voice of temptation that leads us away from God and into the chaos of violence.

During these Lenten gatherings in Nevada, we hear the Word of God invite us again to reject the temptations of violence and the voices of despair, doubt, and domination. We hear the command to remain faithful to the God of peace so that we can walk publicly into the culture of violence and, like Jesus, announce God's reign of nonviolence.

At one peace gathering in the Nevada desert several years ago, the late Archbishop Dom Helder Camara of Brazil called the desert "a good friend." Indeed, the desert is a place of solitude, silence, simplicity, and peace—the place where God lives. It is a place of temptation but also blessing. In the desert we are tempted to power, prestige, and possessions, but it is there, too, that we can claim our baptismal calling to be God's beloved, to trust wholeheartedly in God, and to worship our God.

In the school of the desert, we learn to pray. We learn to sit in silence, to cultivate solitude, to listen to God, to resist the demons of violence, despair, doubt and domination, and to embrace faith, hope, and love. There we receive the inner peace of God. The desert is the school where God disarms our hearts and teaches us a spirituality of nonviolence. It is the place where God prepares us to share Christ's crucifixion and resurrection.

The Gospels invite us to accompany Jesus on his journey of nonviolence from the desert to the cross. They urge us to make his journey our own journey. Jesus' public life begins with his baptism and his lonely days of temptation in the desert. After hearing God call him his beloved Son, Jesus feels pushed by the Holy Spirit into the desert. As he walks alone into that desolate terrain, he confronts the demons of violence that tempt him to despair, doubt, and domination. After he refuses their seductive lure, angels appear and minister to him. Renewed in strength, Jesus goes forward to proclaim the coming of God's nonviolent reign and to receive the world's bitter rejection.

This is our journey as well. In faith, we walk with Jesus individually and communally into the desert—there to confront our own inner violence and be disarmed by God so that we might go forward and struggle for justice and peace even unto death and resurrection. As we accompany Jesus in the desert, he shows us how we cave in to the demons of violence, how we can resist the traps of death, and how we can walk the road of nonviolence.

According to Matthew and Luke, Jesus is tempted three times during his desert fast. First, the tempter says, "If you are the Son of God, command that these stones become loaves of bread." Jesus responds by quoting Scripture: "It is written, 'One does not live by bread alone, / but by every word that comes forth from the mouth of God'" (Matthew 4:3–4).

Notice that the tempter begins his attacks on Jesus with the taunt, "If you are the Son of God." Throughout his life, Jesus' identity is challenged—even to his last day, when he is taunted by Herod, Pilate, and those who pass by as he dies on the cross. Likewise for us, the voice of temptation in today's culture begins by challenging our identities as the beloved sons and daughters of God, the nonviolent followers of Jesus. "Who do you think you are?" the world asks. "If you are a child of God, a person of justice and peace, do something. Prove it. Use your power as the empires use power to control, to kill, to play God. Give us results now. Be successful, be effective. Make a difference here and now. Be relevant—otherwise, you cannot be who you think you are." This is the voice of despair.

The first temptation to violence is the temptation to despair. In desperation, it cries out, "Quick! Do something. You are on your own. You have no food, no security. There is no hope. You must take care of yourself." It renounces patient trust in God and relies on its own power which, in the end, amounts to nothing. While despair pushes us to inhuman, empty solutions, hope leads us to attend to every word from the mouth of God.

In the face of the temptation to despair, Jesus remains human and refuses to give in to the magic of instant, inhuman solutions, for he knows that no one can turn stones into bread. Rather, Jesus listens for the voice of God that spoke to him at his baptism. As a true contemplative, Jesus' quiet, patient trust in God gives him hope. He is hungry but he does not panic or despair. He remains focused on God.

Like Jesus, we are tempted by the culture to change stones to bread, to bring about tangible results. But Jesus calls us back to the Scriptures and urges us not to rely on our own powers but on God and God's word, for it is God who does all the changing and brings all the results. It is God who makes the difference, not us. We are called not to be successful but faithful to God and God's word, which works slowly, humanly, peacefully—not inhumanly, violently, and forcibly, like the empire. We are not called to be powerful but powerless, instruments only of the nonviolent power of God, God's word. We are not called to be relevant but as irrelevant as Jesus—hungry in the desert, dying on the cross. We take up the effectiveness of the cross which, as far as the culture is concerned, is complete lunacy, an absurd failure.

To do this, we live by every utterance that comes from the mouth of God. We listen carefully for the voice of God, attend to God's word, and take that word seriously. God's word transforms us and, through us, the world. God's word is the wisdom of nonviolence that beckons us along the path of peace and love. Fidelity to this word, this life of contemplative listening, keeps us hopeful.

Next the tempter takes Jesus to the Temple in Jerusalem and says, "If you are the Son of God, throw yourself down. For it is written: '[God] will command his angels concerning you' / and 'with their hands they will support you, / lest you dash your foot against a stone.'" Jesus responds, "Again it is written, 'You should not put the Lord, your God, to the test'" (Matthew 4:6–7).

This second temptation of violence is the temptation to doubt, the voice that says that God cannot be trusted. Jesus is tempted to doubt God's abiding love and God's way of nonviolence. He is challenged to test whether or not God is really trustworthy, and whether or not nonviolence works.

But Jesus refuses to doubt God. He will not give in to the faithlessness that leads to violence and self-destruction; rather, he chooses to remain faithful. He knows that when we doubt God's abiding presence, we give in to the world's chaotic violence.

Doubting God's trustworthiness invariably leads to violence against ourselves and others. In the face of the tempter's attempts to trick the nonviolent Jesus into faithlessness and violence, Jesus trusts God, whether he's hungry in the desert or dying on the cross. Thus he does not do violence to himself or reject the way of nonviolence. His faith in God is the foundation of his nonviolence.

But the world tells us that God should not be trusted. It attacks our faith in God and God's loving kindness, pushing us to reject God's way of nonviolence. The culture tells us that God does not care about us, that God is not there for us when we need God and that God, in fact, does not exist. As we abandon our trust in God, we fall prey to the world's violence. "There is no God," the culture insists, "no moral order, no reason to be nonviolent with ourselves or others. Why not step over one another, kill ourselves, or wage war? Nonviolence does not work for God does not exist—and if God does exist, God cannot be trusted."

The culture sows seeds of violence by doubting God and tempting us to self-hatred and self-destruction. In the insanity of violence, where faithlessness deludes us, we are tempted to destroy ourselves and thereby test God's love for us. Once we give in to the voice of despair, the voice of doubt takes us down the spiral of violence to self-hatred and violence toward ourselves.

The culture of violence does not understand God or God's way of nonviolence. It can only urge us to do violence, insisting that we give in to the addiction of violence. But Jesus stands firm. He believes in God and trusts in God, which means he rejects all forms of violence, including self-hatred and self-destruction. "Do not test God," Jesus tells us. "Be at peace with yourself. Treat yourself nonviolently. Trust God and God's way of nonviolence."

The tempter responds to faith in God and steadfast nonviolence by tempting Jesus a third time, offering him all the power in the world.

> The devil took him up to a very high mountain, and showed him all the kingdoms of the world in their magnificence, and he said to [Jesus], "All these I shall give to you, if you will prostrate yourself and worship me." At this, Jesus said to him, "Get away, Satan! It is written:
>
> 'The Lord, your God, shall you worship
> and him alone shall you serve'" (Matthew 4:8–10).

Following the temptations to despair and doubt comes the last temptation: domination, the temptation of imperial power. This temptation summons us to be "number one" in the world, emperor over all, owner of everything, in control of everyone, in charge of life itself. It is the temptation to be God—and it comes with a price: the loss of our souls. It requires the worship of false gods, the idols of death.

As we give in to this last temptation, we try to dominate the world. In our attempts to maintain our imperial domination, we resort to the violence of militarism and nuclear weapons. We stop worshiping God and begin worshiping the false gods of violence.

Jesus rejects the temptation to dominate the world and spurns the way of empire, saying, "Get away, Satan!" "Satan" was often a code word used to describe the Roman Empire, which persecuted and killed members of the early church. Jesus and the early Christian community resist the empire and its domination over others. They refuse to worship Caesar, who considers himself to be god and orders that he be addressed as "my Lord and my God" and the "savior of the world."

Instead, Jesus invites us to serve one another, to love our enemies, to show compassion and mercy to one another, and to worship the living God as he does. Because Jesus turns his back on the world's way of domination, the empire rejects him and eventually kills him. The gospel invites us, likewise, to reject the way of domination and empire, and to worship the God of service, compassion, and nonviolence.

This last temptation questions our basic patriotic presuppositions. Our country prides itself on being "number one" in the world. As the world's policeman and economic tyrant, we try to possess and control all the king-doms of the world—from Iraq and Yugoslavia to Nicaragua and El Salvador. As we do this, however, we also find ourselves worshiping the false gods of violence. Although we claim to worship the living God, in reality we wor-ship the idolatrous weapons we have created to protect our domination over the world's resources. As our militarism insures our economic domi-nation over the poor, we gain the world and lose our souls to the forces of death.

The gospel, however, urges us to do homage to God and God alone—a worship that is not compatible with domination over others. Whereas domination and violence require worship of the instruments of violence—from the gun to the bomb—and the placing of our faith, hope, and trust in our weapons, the gospel invites us to reject the spirituality of empire and its practice of idolatry. It calls us to let go of imperial control—to dismantle our nuclear and conventional arsenals, to relinquish our grasp on the world's resources—that we might accept our powerlessness and turn back to God.

Jesus summons us to the spirituality of nonviolence, to place our trust and security in God. As we learn from Jesus the way of powerlessness, humility, voluntary poverty, and suffering love, we worship the living God. Like the early Christians, we resist the empire and topple its idols. We turn away from the temptations to despair, doubt, and domination, and be-come people of contemplative nonviolence. We learn to live in peace with one another, sharing our resources and welcoming all people equally into the human circle. Together we seek God's reign of justice and peace.

Jesus rejects the temptations to violence—the voices of despair, doubt, and domination—and, in the end, God's angels come and minister to him. "Then the devil left him and, behold, angels came and ministered to him" (Matthew 4:11). In the same way, when we stand firm in faith and nonvio-lence and resist the temptations of the world's violence as Jesus did, God sends the angels of peace to console us as well. We are affirmed and strength-ened for the journey.

The gospel portrait of Jesus' struggle in the desert sums up the inner spiritual struggle that is at the root of Christian nonviolence. Like Jesus, we are summoned to reject violence and its fallout of despair, doubt, and domination, and to trust in God and God's way of nonviolence. If we reject the voices of violence, we will be ministered to by the angels of nonviolence. But even more, the gospel invites us to become the voice of faith and nonviolence to one another, to encourage the Christ in one another to walk the way of nonviolence.

Thus in the desert, we are invited to choose sides. We can be the worldly voice that tempts Christ and others, or we can be the angels who minister to Christ and those who walk the way of nonviolence. We can join the clamoring voices of despair, doubt, and domination in the world, or we can join the ministering angels who encourage Jesus on his journey of nonviolence.

Once we choose, as Christ did, to embrace powerlessness and dependence on God, nonviolence and trust in God, and service and worship of God—once we reject the ways of the world—we open ourselves to the possibility of crucifixion, for empires and imperial states do not take nonviolent resistance lightly. They fight back. They persecute, arrest, imprison, torture, and kill those who oppose them. Our inner resistance to the temptations of violence in the desert prepares us for public, nonviolent resistance to imperial violence in our own modern-day Jerusalems.

If we take up the journey of nonviolence with Christ, from the desert to the cross and beyond to resurrection, we shall encounter God's angels— as Christ did—not only in the desert but on the Mount of Transfiguration, in the Garden of Gethsemane, and in the tomb. They will encourage us to continue the journey of nonviolence. Like Jesus, we will be able to walk out of the desert into our hometown communities filled with faith, hope, and love—ready to announce God's word of peace.

chapter three

THE MISSION

[Jesus] came to Nazareth, where he had grown up, and went according to his custom into the synagogue on the sabbath day. He stood up to read and was handed a scroll of the prophet Isaiah. He unrolled the scroll and found the passage where it was written:

> *"The Spirit of the Lord is upon me*
> *because he has anointed me*
>   *to bring good news to the poor.*
> *He has sent me to proclaim liberty to captives*
> *and recovery of sight to the blind,*
>   *to let the oppressed go free,*
> *and to proclaim a year acceptable to the Lord."*

Rolling up the scroll, he handed it back to the attendant and sat down, and the eyes of all in the synagogue looked intently at him. He said to them, "Today this scripture passage is fulfilled in your hearing."... When the people in the synagogue heard this, they were all filled with fury. They rose up, drove him out of the town, and led him to the brow of the hill on which their town had been built, to hurl him down headlong. But he passed through the midst of them and went away.
(Luke 4:16–21, 28–30)

On fire with love for God and God's reign, Jesus walks out of the desert and goes immediately to his own people in his hometown synagogue to announce his mission. There he reads the prophet Isaiah's revolutionary call for justice and liberation for the poor, and announces that today, in their hearing, the Scripture is fulfilled.

At first the people are dazzled, but questions quickly arise. Who would dare such a claim? This guy, the son of the carpenter, makes true Isaiah's dream of justice? He fulfills the Scriptures? Understandably, the worship service breaks up in argument and yelling and, although the people try to kill Jesus, his promise remains. Because he imagines it, dreams it, announces it, and lives it, Jesus fulfills the prophet's dream of justice.

The key to Jesus' dramatic announcement lies in the text of Isaiah itself. Jesus is not the prime mover here; the Spirit of God is. Jesus simply tells his townspeople that the Spirit of God rests upon him. In baptism, the Spirit came upon him and he heard God call him "my beloved." The Spirit of God then drove him into the desert to fast and pray, and now the Spirit of God sends him forth on a specific mission: to bring good news to the poor, to announce justice and liberation to captives.

Luke's Gospel focuses Jesus' mission specifically on the poor and dis-enfranchised: Jesus will bring liberty to captives, recovery of sight to the blind, and freedom to the oppressed. He calls for a year of jubilee, the year prescribed in the Book of Leviticus (see 25:8 ff), in which wealth is redis-tributed equally so that the poor are no longer poor and the rich are no longer rich. In this year of jubilee, the rich relinquish their extra homes, food, medicine, land, possessions, and money. The poor receive the basic necessities of life. Class distinctions between the rich and the poor fall down. Jesus sides with the poor and oppressed and comes to fulfill their dreams of justice and liberation. In other words, his mission is the mission of the poor and the oppressed. His life work is nothing less than a perma-nent, nonviolent revolution.

The prophet Isaiah's words would have been read periodically in the synagogue but they would probably have been dismissed by the religious elite as utopian rhetoric. "They are not meant to be taken literally," the Pharisees would have taught. Then, suddenly, Jesus announces that not only are these words to be taken literally, but they are being fulfilled in the congregation's hearing.

Jesus applies the Scripture's call for justice to the present-day realities of injustice, saying that Elijah did not appear to the faithless of Israel, but to a widow in enemy territory; that the lepers in Israel were not healed by the prophet but by a leper from among the hated Syrians. Then, when Jesus pointedly declares, "You have failed to enact this Word of God, and because you have not sought justice for the poor and oppressed, God has blessed your hated enemies," the pious, religious congregation explodes with anger and violence. Feeling insulted by Jesus' political accusations, the devout congregation screams, "How dare he ruin our liturgy by speaking of God consorting with the enemy and implying that we are not on God's side in the pursuit of justice."

Luke describes the transformation of a religious congregation into a murderous mob: The people are filled with fury; they rise up as one; they drive Jesus out of town; they lead him to the brow of hill; they intend to hurl him over the cliff. How do the faithful respond to Jesus' call for justice? They try to kill him! His words unmask their murderous hearts, their allegiance to structural injustice, and their hostility toward their enemies. Jesus exposes them; they are not people of prayer or faith, and they will never accept Isaiah's mission or Jesus' gift of social healing. Rather, these devout people benefit from the empire's oppression of the poor, its imprisonment of captives, its marginalization of outsiders, and its class divisions that keep the land and economic resources in their pious, elite hands.

According to Luke, God's reign of justice has come to earth in the person of Jesus. In Jesus, God proclaims good news to the poor, liberates the captives, heals the blind, sets the oppressed free, and proclaims a jubilee year. Luke points out the duty of the congregation in Jesus' day—and in our own day. He summons us to put God's reign of justice into action today, right now, in our own hearing of the gospel story. We, too, are to proclaim good news to the poor, to liberate the captives, to heal the blind, to set the oppressed free, and to proclaim a jubilee year. As Jesus' disciples, we carry out his mission of justice, seeking to fulfill Isaiah's dream even, like Jesus, at risk of our lives.

The Gospel offers us a choice: We can join Jesus' mission or we can reject it, as the congregation in the Nazareth synagogue did two thousand years ago. We can risk our lives proclaiming the good news to the poor, releasing the imprisoned, giving sight to the blind, offering liberty to the oppressed, and seeking justice, economic conversion, disarmament, and the transformation of society. Or—we can respond to Jesus' demand for justice for the poor like the angry crowd: with anger, resentment, and violence. Hypocritically, we can continue to attend religious services while benefiting from systemic injustice, the oppression of the world's poor, and the business of war. Through our silent complicity with the world's violence, we can try to kill Christ again.

Religious congregations gather every day for prayer and Scripture reading without taking to heart Jesus' command to seek justice and make peace. More often than not our churches promote personal piety but not the pursuit of economic justice and social liberation. They do not rock the ship of state. Rarely, in fact, do church officials proclaim good news to the poor or denounce the injustice that kills the poor. Rather, they roll on with the ship of state, a Titanic sailing to its doom.

Christian church congregations by and large tolerate the culture's bad news to the poor: its welfare cuts, school closings, discontinuation of needed service programs, unlivable wages, inadequate healthcare, environmental degradation, and worse. We—the people in those congregations—walk past the homeless and make other people homeless. We allow forty thousand women and children to die each day from hunger and hunger-related disease around the world. We do not seek the release of the imprisoned but rather, support the government's construction of scores of new prisons; we vote for measures to make incarceration as painful as possible and support the death penalty by an overwhelming majority around the country. We do not seek to heal the blind; rather, we turn our backs as healthcare costs skyrocket out of the reach of the poor. We do not demand liberty for the world's poor because we middle-class churchgoers benefit economically from their oppression. We push women, children, the hungry, the home-less, the imprisoned, African-Americans, Hispanics, Asian-Americans, gays, lesbians, the elderly, the disabled, the unborn, and those with AIDS to the margins—and we keep them there. Finally, we do not call for economic conversion and disarmament, much less put the jubilee year into practice. We do not give our houses, cars, bank accounts, and other possessions to the poor, as God demands. Rather, we cling to our possessions and climb over one another in pursuit of money. By silently allowing injustice to rage around us, we oppose God's transformation of society into a more just, more humane reality. Like the congregation in Nazareth, we set aside texts like this passage as quaint biblical stories that do not apply to our situation.

Jesus, on the other hand, stakes his life on this mission of justice and expects his followers to do the same. He wants us to spend our days fulfill-ing Isaiah's dream that he embraces as his own. When we were baptized, we, too, were anointed by the Holy Spirit. We, too, were sent out to bring good news to the poor, liberty to captives, recovery of sight to the blind, and the proclamation of a jubilee year of justice. If we are going to follow Jesus, Luke explains, we have to embrace Isaiah's cause as our own—and we have to be prepared for the controversy and trouble that inevitably follows. People will be threatened and offended by our commitment to justice and peace, and they will go to no limit to stop us. Nonetheless, the mission remains.

To engage in the nonviolent revolution that Jesus begins is to risk the cross—a fate foretold for him on that first day in Nazareth. Yet, realizing that his message has been rejected, Jesus continues with his mission—and he wants us to do the same. He hopes that we will give our lives for the scripture's fulfillment. "You will be hated and feared because you seek justice and peace," he tells us, "but I want you to pursue this vision, come what may." Like Jesus, we will face hostility and opposition from our own religious communities and from the Church itself. We may even undergo harassment, ostracism, alienation, arrest, imprisonment, and death. But if we do, we will have the consolation of knowing that we served the mission of Jesus, God's reign of justice. Nothing is more important.

Many people have faithfully fulfilled Jesus' mission. God continues to send prophets who announce Jesus' vision of justice, liberation, and non-violent revolution. For example, God sent Dorothy Day, founder of the Catholic Worker community, to stand with the poor, denounce war, and call for nuclear disarmament. God sent Oscar Romero, Archbishop of San Salvador, to walk among the disenfranchised and denounce the death-squad government that eventually shot him while he celebrated Mass. God sent Martin Luther King, Jr., to demand equality and civil rights for all people, economic justice for the poor, and an end to U.S. militaristic expansionism. God sent Mohandas Gandhi to resist racism in South Africa, rebel against British imperialism in India, and call humanity to nonviolence. God sent Jean Donovan, Ita Ford, Maura Clarke, and Dorothy Kazel— ordinary North American churchwomen who changed their lives and pursued the jubilee vision of justice—to offer good news to the poor, to heal the blind, and to liberate the oppressed in Central America.

Likewise, God wants us to fulfill this biblical vision. God sends us right into our own hometowns to call for justice for the poor and to denounce systemic injustice. As we let go of our ambitions, enter the world of the poor, speak out against injustice, and call for justice and disarmament, we can anticipate our own modern-day version of the cross. We can expect disapproval and persecution from those around us, especially those within the Christian community.

But we know the end of the story. If we risk suffering and death with Jesus for the sake of biblical justice, we will share in its fulfillment and enter his resurrection in God's reign of peace. Jesus was raised from the dead and, as we share in his struggle for justice and peace, so will we share in his resurrection victory.

chapter four

THE CALL

*As he was walking by the Sea of Galilee, [Jesus] saw two brothers, Simon
who is called Peter, and his brother Andrew, casting a net into the sea;
they were fishermen. He said to them, "Come after me, and I will make
you fishers of men [and women]." At once they left their nets and followed him. He walked along from there and saw two other brothers,
James, the son of Zebedee, and his brother John. They were in a boat,
with their father Zebedee, mending their nets. He called them, and immediately they left their boat and their father and followed him. (Matthew
4:18–22)*

After Jesus emerges from the waters of baptism and the temptations
of the desert, he forms a community by calling people to become
his disciples. "Come after me," he says to the ordinary men and women of
his day and, one by one, they drop everything, leave their relations, renounce their livelihood, and walk with Jesus. They are so attracted to
Jesus—his hopeful message, his healing presence, and his revolutionary
nonviolence—that they abandon their former lives and devote themselves
completely to him.

In our own confusing times, it is hard to imagine the personal cha-
risma that could summon us to renounce our families and livelihoods in
radical discipleship. Yet, a handful of world figures in our own century
have drawn widespread devotion, people like Mohandas Gandhi, Martin
Luther King, Jr., Dorothy Day, Mother Teresa, the Dalai Lama, and Nelson
Mandela. None of these charismatic leaders, however, invited others to be
their disciples, like Jesus did. Jesus wanted a community of followers and
friends to walk with him on his journey of nonviolence and to carry on his
mission of love and peace after his death.

23

The word *disciple* derives from Latin and means "one who learns." In the Gospels, both John the Baptist and the Pharisees have disciples. Jesus, too, is portrayed as having disciples, both a large gathering of disciples (see Matthew 5:1 and Luke 6:17, 19:37) and a small intimate group of disciples, sometimes explicitly called "the Twelve." Luke, for example, refers to a large group of seventy or seventy-two men and women sent on mission by Jesus as his disciples. Later, in the Acts of the Apostles, all the Christians of Jerusalem are referred to as "disciples" (see Acts 6:1–7).

Each Gospel describes the invitation to the first disciples. Matthew and Mark, for example, summarize the initial call of the fishermen brothers, Simon and Andrew and James and John, with the poetic invitation: "Come after me, and I will make you fishers of men [and women]" (Matthew 4:19 and Mark 1:17). Scripture scholar Ched Myers points out that the Evangelists refer here to Jeremiah 16:16, where Yahweh promises to send out fishers to catch and hunters to hunt the faithless—the idolatrous people of Israel. The prophets Amos (see 4:2) and Ezekiel (see 29:4) speak of the "hooking of fish" as a judgment upon the rich and oppressors. In the tradition of the prophets before him, Jesus invites the poor to join him in his nonviolent struggle to overturn the existing order of imperial power, privilege, and injustice. Later, Matthew and Mark also record the call to Matthew (or Levi), the tax collector, with the direct command: "Follow me" (Matthew 9:9; Mark 2:14). Although an outcast derided by the people, this tax collector shares a meal with Jesus and receives the invitation to follow.

Luke paints an even more detailed portrait of the call to discipleship in his scene of Peter's call. Jesus uses Peter's boat to speak to the crowds on the shore and, afterwards, orders Peter to go "out into deep water and lower your nets for a catch" (Luke 5:4). Although he and his coworkers had been fishing unsuccessfully all night, Peter grudgingly obeys. Then, after catching more fish than ever before, he suddenly realizes his own unworthiness and pride in the presence of Jesus, falls at the feet of Jesus, and confesses his sin. In reply, Jesus says, "Do not be afraid; from now on you will be catching men [and women]" (5:10).

John's Gospel, on the other hand, presents Peter's call to discipleship at the end of the story, after Peter denies knowing Jesus, after Jesus is executed and rises. Jesus tells Peter that "when you were younger, you used to dress yourself and go where you wanted; but when you grow old, you will stretch out your hands, and someone else will dress you and lead you where you do not want to go." The narrator then goes on to explain that Jesus says this to Peter to signify "by what kind of death he would glorify God. And when he had said this, he said to him, 'Follow me'" (21:18–19).

After an opening prologue, the Gospel of John actually begins with a description of the call to discipleship. When he sees Jesus walk by, John the Baptist tells his own disciples, "Behold, the Lamb of God." Then, when the disciples set off to follow Jesus, Jesus turns and asks, "What are you looking for?" In turn, the disciples ask, "Where are you staying?" to which Jesus replies, "Come, and you will see." The next day, we are told, Jesus "finds" Philip in Galilee and says to him, "Follow me" (1:36, 38–39, 43).

One gets the impression that Jesus walks through life inviting all sorts of people to follow him and that, occasionally, some do. Along the way, he reiterates his requirement of complete commitment even unto death. The disciple he seeks, for example, must renounce everything, as Luke records:

> "If anyone wishes to come after me, [they] must deny [themselves] and take up [their] cross daily and follow me. For whoever wishes to save [their] life will lose it, but whoever loses [their] life for my sake will save it. What profit is there for one to gain the whole world yet lose or forfeit [themselves]?" (Luke 9:23–25)

To highlight the urgent demands of discipleship, Luke records three encounters between Jesus and potential followers:

> As they were proceeding on their journey someone said to him, "I will follow you wherever you go." Jesus answered him, "Foxes have dens and birds of the sky have nests, but the Son of Man has nowhere to rest his head." And to another he said, "Follow me." But he replied, ". . . [L]et me go first and bury my father." But he answered him, "Let the dead bury their dead. But you, go and proclaim the kingdom of God." And another said, "I will follow you, Lord, but first let me say farewell to my family at home." (To him) Jesus said, "No one who sets a hand to the plow and looks to what was left behind is fit for the kingdom of God" (Luke 9:57–62).

Jesus does not romanticize his way of life. He is homeless, so his followers, too, can expect to wander the earth as pilgrims on a mission to proclaim God's nonviolent reign. Notice the potential disciple, for example, who begs off to bury his father. This request does not mean that the man's father has died; rather, custom dictates that the oldest son must remain at home until his father dies so that he can bury the father. Jesus dismisses this sentimental, traditional obedience to parents: "Go and proclaim God's reign," he commands. To the last potential disciple in this passage, Jesus insists that his mission has a life-and-death urgency. The end of the old world is at hand—and so is God's reign. Get with it, stay with it, and don't give up.

Luke then tells us that after these encounters, Jesus appoints "seventy (-two) others whom he sent ahead of him in pairs to every town and place he intended to visit." Jesus tells these disciples:

> "Go on your way; behold, I am sending you like lambs among wolves. Carry no money bag, no sack, no sandals; and greet no one along the way. Into whatever house you enter, first say, 'Peace to this household.' If a peaceful person lives there, your peace will rest on him . . . [C]ure the sick . . . and say to them, 'The kingdom of God is at hand for you'" (Luke 10:1, 3–6, 9).

Jesus likens the disciples to the exiled Israelites wandering in the desert. They are people of peace. Because nonviolence is the linchpin of his life and message, Jesus intends it to be the hallmark of his disciples as well.

Myers contrasts Jesus' call to discipleship with the Pharisees' devoted students:

> Mark's call-paradigm contrasts sharply with the traditional method of rabbinic recruitment. Normally the student sought the teacher and followed only for as long as it took to attain rabbinic status himself. The call of Jesus, however, is absolute, disrupting the lives of potential recruits, promising them only a "school" from which there is no graduation. This "first" call to discipleship in Mark is an urgent, uncompromising invitation to "break with business as usual." The world is coming to an end, for those who choose to follow. The kingdom has dawned, and it is identified with the discipleship adventure.[1]

The Gospels do not romanticize discipleship; the fact is, disciples drop everything, renounce their livelihood, leave everyone, and follow Jesus completely. There is no halfway, part-time, temporary discipleship. It's all or nothing. Jesus expects his disciples to join his nonviolent revolution and to risk their lives for it. His disciples will heal the sick, exorcise demons, build community, proclaim God's reign, practice nonviolence, carry the cross, keep watch with him, pray with him, share the eucharistic meal and, most importantly, die and rise with him—to remain with him forever.

Jesus practices revolutionary nonviolence, and accepting his call to become his disciple puts you in serious danger. After all, to live a long life in first-century Palestine, you play it safe, stay out of trouble, and mind your own business. You obey the rules of the empire and its religious subservients, the scribes and the Pharisees. You do what you are told. Those who espouse revolutionary politics, the Zealots, wage guerilla warfare against the Roman imperial outposts and, when caught, are tortured and crucified. The Gospels tell how the disciples, knowing that Jesus' actions and teachings are illegal, slowly realize the implications of their allegiance. They could be arrested and executed as revolutionaries—and they are to respond without violent retaliation or revenge but with love, forgiveness, and peace. What had they gotten themselves into?

In keeping with his nonviolence, Jesus does not force anyone to follow him. People walk away from him. In the end, of course, they all flee from him. His way of revolutionary nonviolence means almost certain arrest and execution in his time. Nonetheless, he goes ahead to the cross, rises from the dead, and continues to seek disciples to join him on his campaign of nonviolence and liberation. He promises trouble and persecution—but he also promises hundreds of new sisters and brothers and the fullness of life, an eternal communion with him. Those who follow and put his teachings into practice, he promises, will be "blessed."

When the imperial troops catch Jesus, all the male disciples abandon him. According to all four Gospels, only a few women disciples remain faithful, and they do so from a distance. At his resurrection, Jesus appears to these faithful women and then to the entire community. Filled with his spirit, these women and men set out to light the world on fire with his story and to call others to his discipleship of nonviolence.

In the first three centuries, discipleship to Christ ensured a death warrant, and these early Christians were regularly killed for professing Christ as their Lord and Master. Baptism itself was an act of nonviolent civil disobedience to the imperial authority. In fact, the newly baptized were often immediately executed by Roman soldiers. From the disciples' perspective, however, their death warrant ensured new life.

What does it mean to be a disciple of Jesus today? Discipleship today still involves risk and personal upheaval. It involves the relinquishment of our job security, personal comforts, family protection, and allegiance to the culture. Discipleship to Jesus requires solidarity with the poor, adherence to nonviolence, love for everyone, community life, public action for justice, contemplative prayer, eucharistic celebration, and worship of the God of Life. It opens the possibility of failure, loss of reputation, irrelevance, loneliness, pain, suffering, persecution, and imprisonment. It not only calls for an alternative personal, social, and economic way of life, but demands that we give up our very lives to accompany Jesus as he continues to carry the cross today in the nonviolent struggle for justice and peace.

As Dietrich Bonhoeffer wrote in his landmark work, *The Cost of Discipleship,* shortly before he was executed by the Nazis, our discipleship has become comfortable and cheap. We rarely glimpse, at least in First World America, the radical discipleship that the Gospels demand. Rather, we have become safe, silent, somnolent churchgoers. Discipleship to Jesus has lost its edge; it is no longer illegal. It is, in fact, legal, mainstream, and expected of us by the dominant culture. It is far from revolutionary. It has become a private, personal affair with few social ramifications.

Just as Christian disciples obeyed Hitler and incinerated millions of human beings; enforced racist apartheid on South African blacks; and supported disappearances, torture, and executions by death-squad soldiers in El Salvador, Guatemala, Argentina, and elsewhere, so do Christian disciples today develop and maintain weapons of mass destruction at the Pentagon, the Strategic Air Command Base, and in Trident submarines, missile silos, weapons stations, and military bases across the country. People have no trouble supporting these weapons of mass destruction while professing faith in the Christ. Their discipleship to Jesus is removed from their military work, nationalism, and civic responsibility. They privatize their faith and, in the process, become disciples of the culture, not the Christ.

Yet, a close reading of the Gospels challenges us to make our discipleship to Jesus count. It dares us to let our lives be disrupted by Jesus' vision. Bonhoeffer renamed the Christian vocation for our times as "costly discipleship." If we do not feel the cost of discipleship, we have yet to become true disciples, he wrote shortly before his execution.

Following Jesus today in a land of nuclear weapons, rampant racism, and widespread economic injustice means actively going against our culture of violence. As the culture promotes violence, we promote Jesus' nonviolence. As the culture calls for war, we call for Jesus' peace. As the culture supports racism, sexism, and classism, we demand Jesus' vision of equality, community, and reconciliation. As the culture insists on vengeance and execution, we pray with Jesus for forgiveness and compassion. As the culture summons us to be successful, to make money, to have a career, to get to the top, and to be number one, we race in the opposite direction and go with Jesus into voluntary poverty, powerlessness, humility, suffering, and death.

Discipleship to Jesus, according to the gospel, requires that we love our enemies, demand justice for the poor, seek liberation of the oppressed, visit the sick and the imprisoned, topple the idols of death, resist militarism, reject consumerism, dismantle racism, create community, beat swords into plowshares, and worship the God of peace. If we try to engage in these social practices, we will feel the sting of discipleship and the gospel will come alive.

On that day, we will know what it means to be Jesus' disciple.

chapter five

BLESSED ARE THE NONVIOLENT

Blessed are the poor in spirit,
  for theirs is the kingdom of heaven.
Blessed are they who mourn,
  for they will be comforted.
Blessed are the meek,
  for they will inherit the land.
Blessed are those who hunger and thirst for righteousness,
  for they will be satisfied.
Blessed are the merciful,
  for they will be shown mercy.
Blessed are the clean of heart,
  for they will see God.
Blessed are the peacemakers,
  for they will be called children of God.
Blessed are they who are persecuted for the sake of righteousness,
  for theirs is the kingdom of heaven.
Blessed are you when they insult you and persecute you and utter every
kind of evil against you (falsely) because of me. Rejoice and be glad, for
your reward will be great in heaven. Thus they persecuted the prophets
who were before you. (Matthew 5:3–12)

A few months before I entered the Jesuits, in the summer of 1982, I flew to Israel to make a pilgrimage through the Holy Land, to walk in the footsteps of Jesus. On the day I arrived, Israel invaded Lebanon. As I stepped off the plane and soldiers carrying machine guns searched me, I found myself in the middle of full-scale warfare.

After nearly a month traveling around Israel, I spent my last week camping along the beautiful Sea of Galilee in the north. There were no tourists, so I spent the days outdoors, swimming in the cool water, watching the sun rise and set, and quietly meditating on the Sermon on the Mount. Each day, I sat in the small stone Chapel of the Beatitudes, which stands on a hilltop overlooking the sea, and where the beatitudes are inscribed along the church's eight-sided walls. One afternoon, I read the words slowly and carefully: "Blessed are the poor. Blessed are those who mourn. Blessed are the meek. Blessed are those who hunger and thirst for justice. Blessed are the merciful. Blessed are the pure in heart. Blessed are the peacemakers. Blessed are those persecuted for the sake of justice, for my name's sake." Then, as I walked out onto the balcony overlooking the Sea of Galilee and the blue sky above, it suddenly dawned on me: Jesus is serious.

I looked up at the sky and said to God, "Are you trying to tell me something? Do you want me to hunger and thirst for justice? Do you want me to be a peacemaker? Do you want me to love even my enemies? All right," I declared, "I promise to work for peace and justice for the rest of my life—on one condition: if you give me a sign!"

All of a sudden, I heard loud explosions and sonic booms as two Israeli jets swooped down from the sky, appearing right over the Sea of Galilee and heading straight at me! They flew directly over me and, a few moments later, dropped bombs along the Lebanon border. Trembling, I looked up. "Okay, God, I'll work for peace and justice," I said, "and I'll never ask for a sign again."

Now of course, many years later, I know that people of faith do not ask for signs. At that moment, however, I saw the reality of war and death in our world as if for the first time. Even more powerfully, at that moment in history, in Galilee, at the Mount itself, I heard Jesus as if for the first time saying what he still says today: "The God of peace wants you to live, not kill; to spend your life rooted in God, living life to the full, promoting life for all, serving all those in need, loving even your enemies, and working to stop war and injustice."

Ever since that call in Galilee, the beatitudes have stood as guideposts on my journey. They summon me, like Buddha's Noble Eightfold Path, to that promised blessing of God's reign. They direct me, like a map, along the way of nonviolence. Yet, whenever I think I have them nailed down, I discover that they have receded once again into the distance—or rather, my heart has grown colder and I have strayed far from the noble path of nonviolence.

As I ponder God's spirituality of nonviolence, I marvel at the dramatic contrast the beatitudes present to our culture's spirituality of violence. The culture's anti-beatitudes begin, first and foremost, with the basic rule: "Blessed are the rich; the reign of the world is theirs." The rich rule the world; the poor get poorer and disappear. This is old news, of course. As the culture hypnotizes us to pursue money, possessions, power, and prestige, Jesus turns the values of the world upside-down and calls us to the economics of God's reign. Blessed are the poor for, although they have nothing in the eyes of the world, they have one thing the rich do not have: the reign of God.

"Blessed are those who cause others to mourn," the nations proclaim. "Blessed are those who kill, who support killing, who wage war, who pay taxes for killing, who allow nuclear weapons and war preparations to exist, who legalize the murder of people on death row." In other words, "Blessed are those who do not mourn or grieve." In their time of trial, however, they shall be alone. They shall not be comforted.

"Blessed are the violent," the culture declares. "Blessed are the proud, the arrogant, the powerful, those who dominate others, those who oppress the poor, those who support the systems of domination." They supposedly own everything—yet, they shall inherit nothing.

"Blessed are those who hunger and thirst for injustice," the system tells us, "for the reign of this world is theirs." The world belongs to those who support, promote, and benefit from injustice, from the sufferings of the poor. Because of their desire for injustice, they shall not be satisfied. They shall not find meaning to their lives.

"Blessed are those who show no mercy," the world insists—no mercy to the victims, to the poor, to women, to children, to the elderly, to the homeless, to social outcasts, to the refugee, to·the hungry, to the enemy, to the unborn, to those on death row. Yet, the world does not tell us the inevitable spiritual consequences of mercilessness: "They shall be shown no mercy."

"Blessed are the war-makers," the military and its chaplains announce. "Blessed are those who support militarism, who pay for weapons, who fund the Pentagon, who march off to war, who stir the embers of patriotism, who make the guns, who keep the myth of 'redemptive' violence aloft. They shall be called the sons and daughters of the idols of death, sons and daughters of the bomb. They are children of the deadly gods of war, not the living God of peace."

Finally, the world declares: "Blessed are those who are not persecuted for justice; who are comfortable, safe, and secure; who do not get involved in the struggle for social change; who remain silent, turn a deaf ear to the cries of the poor, and fund and participate in systemic injustice. The reign of this world is theirs." Again, it fails to explain the spiritual consequence of complicity with systemic injustice: "The reign of God is not theirs."

In the Sermon on the Mount, Jesus teaches that the way of nonviolence is a narrow path that few find, while the road to destruction is wide and many take it. Nonetheless, into the culture of violence, Jesus comes announcing the God of nonviolence and a life-giving spirituality of nonviolence. The beatitudes, we could say, are the primary text, the basic guidelines, of nonviolence. They challenge us to live every facet of nonviolence just as Jesus did.

Jesus begins, "Blessed are the poor in spirit—not the rich, not the powerful, not those in control, but the poor of spirit." The poor in spirit receive the first and greatest blessing—entrance into God's reign. Jesus urges us to let go of our possessions, our power over others, and our prestige, to discover the reign of God in our emptiness. Only in the letting go of everything we possess, to the point of giving our lives for others, do we let go of every trace of violence or domination. This is a great and difficult lesson—the beginning of wisdom.

The poor in spirit have learned this first of all. They understand nonviolence by heart. That is why Jesus begins his life among the poor and calls us to share our lives with them—because God's reign shines first in the midst of the poor, away from the power and glare of the world. As we share our lives with the poor, Jesus explains, they share with us the one thing they have: the reign of God. So the gospel pushes us: Try to live in greater solidarity with the poor; to share personal relationships with poor people; to let go of power, control, and domination; and to taste their poverty of spirit, their powerlessness.

"Blessed are those who mourn," Jesus continues. Millions of people in our world mourn because their loved ones have been killed by war, starvation, or injustice. Do we grieve for those who die in war? for those incinerated by nuclear weapons and bombs? for the sixty thousand who die each day from starvation? Do we allow the sorrow of the world's poor to touch our hearts? Do we look the suffering of the world in the eye and take on the task of ending injustice, or do we turn away in denial and thus postpone our own inevitable confrontation with grief? Jesus promises that, as we mourn the death of our sisters and brothers around the world, God consoles us and we find a peace—even a joy that we did not know possible.

"Blessed are the meek," Jesus teaches, "they shall inherit the earth." Here we discover the biblical word for nonviolence. Although the world praises the violent, the arrogant, and the proud, Jesus invites humility, gentleness, and nonviolence. He challenges us to renounce every form of violence in our hearts and in our world. As we enter into his spirit of creative nonviolence, we receive the blessing of creation itself.

"Blessed are those who hunger and thirst for justice," Jesus insists, "they shall be satisfied." Be passionate for justice, he tells us. In other words, resist injustice with every bone in your body. As the Jesuit martyr from El Salvador, Ignacio Ellacuria, wrote, "Christians and all those who hate injustice are obligated to fight it with every ounce of their strength. They must work for a new world in which greed and selfishness will finally be overcome."

Seeking justice is a constitutive element of our faith, a matter of life and death, and thus a spiritual matter. "How concerned are you about injustice in the world?" the gospel asks. "How much do you crave justice?" Jesus says that to the extent that we struggle for justice, we will find meaning and purpose in our lives. In the struggle itself, Jesus explains, speaking from his own experience, we find true satisfaction.

"Blessed are the merciful; they shall be shown mercy." While we struggle for justice on the one hand, Jesus instructs, we offer mercy with our other hand, especially toward those who have hurt us and seek our forgiveness. Mercy is the very heart of God. In *The Sign of Jonas*, Thomas Merton described God as "Mercy within Mercy within Mercy." "Be as compassionate and as merciful as God," Jesus pleads, "forgiving yourselves and everyone you meet, including those who have killed your loved ones." Sister Helen Prejean exemplifies this mercy as she befriends those on death row and their families, as well as the family members of the victims. The gospel paints the summit of mercy in the crucified Jesus' prayer for forgiveness on those who have killed him (see Luke 23:34). Instead of seeking

retaliation or revenge toward those who hurt us, we, like Jesus, offer forgiveness and compassion. As we share mercy, we sow seeds of mercy that,
on the last day, will wash back over us.

"Blessed are the pure in heart; they shall see God." To be a person of
nonviolence, for Jesus, is to be at peace within ourselves. To live with a
disarmed heart requires contemplation because only through daily intimate prayer can the God of peace disarm our hearts of inner violence.

"While you are proclaiming peace with your lips, be careful to have it
even more fully in your heart," St. Francis advised. As we cultivate nonviolence of the heart, and root all we do in our relationship with the God of
peace, we begin to see God everywhere—in the poor, in the struggle for
justice and peace, in our communities, in the gifts of bread and wine, in
creation itself, in our enemies, in one another. Jesus promises that one day
this pure, heartfelt contemplation will lead us to the beatific vision. We
will see God face to face.

Jesus wants his followers to make peace, to end war, to root out the
conditions for war, and to reconcile with everyone in our families, in our
neighborhoods, in our cities, in our nation, and in the world. Thus he
teaches, "Blessed are the peacemakers." He calls us to make peace by renouncing war and nuclear weapons, by seeking disarmament, by persistently
reconciling with all peoples, and by loving our enemies. Jesus would bring
together people of all races on our city block as well as heal the deep ethnic
divisions in the former Yugoslavia, Rwanda, and Northern Ireland. Such
public peacemaking is hard, of course, and peacemakers like Jesus rarely
live to see the fruit of their work. They usually find themselves misunder-
stood and rejected, if not labeled with every possible epithet. Jesus calls
them the sons and daughters of God.

"Blessed are those persecuted for the sake of justice for my name's
sake. Rejoice and be glad!" This last instruction may be the hardest of all.
Dorothy Day of the Catholic Worker movement noted that we can measure our discipleship by the amount of persecution we undergo. For Jesus,
the greatest blessing comes in suffering for the noble cause of justice and
refusing to retaliate with violence. In that moment, the reign of God is
revealed as unconditional, nonviolent, redemptive love. As we are persecuted for speaking the truth, denouncing injustice, calling for disarmament,
and engaging in direct action for social change, we enter into the final

blessing of Jesus' life: the paschal mystery of cross and resurrection. Then, as we share in the paschal mystery, we not only promote the coming of justice, but we welcome God's reign. We sow the seeds of justice and peace that will one day blossom. As we willingly suffer for justice, refuse to retaliate with further violence, and pursue the truth of justice and peace until our dying breath, we rejoice because we share the lot of the saints, the prophets, the martyrs, and Jesus himself. In this joy, the nonviolent reign of God is at hand.

The beatitudes teach us about the mystery of God. As we experiment with the beatitudes in our lives and plumb the spirituality of nonviolence in our hearts, God does things to us. According to Jesus, God takes the initiative. God responds with blessings, gives us God's reign, consoles us, gives us the earth for an inheritance, satisfies our longings for social justice, bestows mercy upon us, shows God's face to us, calls us God's sons and daughters, gives us joy, and offers us the fullness of life in heaven.

We are blessed indeed.

chapter six

LOVE YOUR ENEMIES

"You have heard that it was said, 'You shall love your neighbor and hate your enemy.' But I say to you, love your enemies, and pray for those who persecute you, that you may be children of your heavenly Father, for he makes his sun rise on the bad and the good, and causes rain to fall on the just and the unjust. For if you love those who love you, what recompense will you have? Do not the tax collectors do the same? And if you greet your brothers only, what is unusual about that? Do not the pagans do the same? So be perfect, just as your heavenly Father is perfect." (Matthew 5:43–48)

The command to love our enemies stands at the center of the Sermon on the Mount, Jesus' life message. Never before in history had anyone suggested such a daring proposal. Today, nearly two thousand years later, Jesus' way of love offers a way out of the world's nightmare of hatred and war. "Love for our enemies," Martin Luther King, Jr. concluded, "is the key to the solution of the problems of the world."[1]

Despite the end of the cold war, our country continues to stockpile weapons of mass destruction and research new ways to kill its enemies on a massive scale. Meanwhile, some thirty-five wars are currently being waged around the world, from the Middle East to the Sudan to Sri Lanka. A plague of violence tears the human family apart: nuclear incinerations on Hiroshima and Nagasaki, bombing raids, nuclear threats, executions, abortions, torture, homelessness, racism, and sexism. Our wars and weapons still have the potential to destroy all of life.

Into this overwhelming violence comes Jesus with a way out: "Love your enemies. Practice the unconditional love of God with all people as you work for justice and peace. Stop killing one another, stop waging war, stop building and maintaining nuclear weapons, and become people of nonviolence. Shower your enemies with heartfelt love. See them as your sisters and brothers, and you will win them over and learn to live at peace with one another. Then you will become like God: peacemakers."

Jesus' alternative to enmity is the persistent, reconciling love of God. He calls us to extend the all-embracing love of God across national boundaries, so that the reconciliation already created by God will be more apparent. This love will disarm all sides and bear the good fruit of peace and justice. In this great love, Jesus calls us to be God's daughters and sons and shows us how to be like God.

As a North American living in the United States, I struggle with this great commandment. Throughout the 1980s, as the United States named the poor of El Salvador its enemy and waged war upon them, my friends and I tried to resist our government's war-making and love the Salvadoran people. In 1985, while living in a Salvadoran refugee camp, I witnessed U.S. bombing raids and visited peacemaking Jesuit priests who were subsequently assassinated for their prophetic truth-telling. I frequently was jailed for prayerfully demonstrating at military bases and offices across the country in an effort to protest U.S. military aid to El Salvador.

In this journey of nonviolent love, I have also sheltered the homeless, advocated for the unborn and those on death row, traveled in missions of solidarity to Iraq, Haiti, the Philippines, Palestine, Nicaragua, and Guatemala, demonstrated against the U.S. bombing of Iraq, and crossed the line at many nuclear weapons installations in acts of nonviolent civil disobedience to call for nuclear disarmament. Along with several friends, I professed a vow of nonviolence to formalize this commitment to nonviolent love. Yet, I wonder; have I been faithful to Jesus' command? Instead of love, have I not often shown self-righteousness, anger, and even hatred for my opponents? I have a long way to go.

On December 7, 1993, three friends joined me in walking onto the Seymour Johnson Air Force Base in Goldsboro, North Carolina, right through the middle of full-scale war games. In the spirit of Isaiah's vision to "beat swords into plowshares" and Jesus' command to love our enemies, the four of us hammered on an F15 fighter bomber. At the time, these F15s were the cutting edge of the U.S. Air Force, had recently killed thousands of Iraqis during the Gulf war, were on alert to bomb Bosnia, and were equipped to carry nuclear weapons. We were immediately surrounded by soldiers armed with machine guns aimed directly at us. "We are unarmed, peaceful people," I said. "We mean you no harm. We are here simply to disarm this weapon of death." For a brief moment, the young soldiers looked quizzically at us, trying to comprehend our action. They then shook their heads angrily and shouted, "You can't do that! This is the real world!" As a result of our actions, we were jailed for between eight to fourteen months. Although the trials and jail-time were difficult and painful, they were also a profound grace. In our prayerful effort to obey Jesus' love command and to call for nuclear disarmament, we experienced the blessings of the beatitudes.

When my friends and family asked, "What difference did it make? How effective was it?" I could only reply that, like all sacramental experiences, our action could not be measured for results. If this was an act of faith, a sharing in Jesus' cross, as we believed it was, then God was present and the results would be in God's hands—better hands than ours. We were simply trying to love our enemies by trying to stop our country's preparations to kill them.

As we learned, the government does not take such egalitarian love lightly. We were labeled criminals and felons for our "crime," which we insisted was no crime at all but a legal enactment of international law and Nuremberg principles. The government, on the other hand, decreed in no uncertain terms that loving our enemies is, in fact, illegal.

If we take Jesus at his word and love our enemies, our lives will be disrupted. Because the world revolves around the presupposition that enemies are for hating and killing, those who cross national boundaries and political expectations will face tremendous opposition and persecution. Perhaps that is why Jesus, immediately after his command to love, commands us to pray for those who persecute us. He knows the political outcome of real enemy love. He wants us to place our persecutors at the heart of our prayer, just as our enemies are the center of our loving attention.

Perhaps we avoid this teaching because there is no easy way to love our enemies. It will not make us popular, win us friends, or advance our careers. It will not benefit anyone—except the lives of our enemies. Indeed, we may never know the results of our efforts to love our enemies, although we may have actually saved lives. We may never know the wars that have been prevented, the longstanding enmity that has been healed, or the long-term international reconciliation that began. Loving our enemies is like faith itself; it is an act of trust in God and in the future. It is an act of hope.

When Matthew and Luke write about this love, they avoid the popular Greek words for love, such as *storge* (referring to family love), *eros* (referring to passionate, physical love), and *philia* (referring to affectionate love between friends and neighbors). Rather, they deliberately use the Greek word *agape,* which is an unconditional, non-retaliatory, sacrificial love toward all humanity. As one Scripture scholar explains, "*Agape* does not mean a feeling of the heart, which we cannot help, and which comes unbidden and unsought; it means a determination of the mind, whereby we achieve this unconquerable goodwill even to those who hurt and injure us. *Agape* is the power to love those whom we do not like and who do not like us."[2] In his first book, *Stride Toward Freedom,* Martin Luther King, Jr. defined *agape:*

> *Agape* is not a weak, passive love. It is love in action. *Agape* is love seeking to preserve and create community. It is insistence on community even when one seeks to break it. *Agape* is a willingness to sacrifice in the interest of mutuality. *Agape* is a willingness to go to any length to restore community. It is a willingness to forgive, not seven times, but seventy times seven to restore community. . . . *Agape* means a recognition of the fact that all life is interrelated. All humanity is involved in a single process, and all men and women are brothers and sisters. . . . When I am commanded to love, I am commanded to restore community, to resist injustice and to meet the needs of my brothers and sisters.[3]

When Jesus commands us, his followers, to show *agape* toward our enemies, he summons us to stretch ourselves beyond the normal expectations of society and to see all humanity with God's own loving eyes. From this all-embracing perspective, we go forward to love those threatened or hurt by our country in the hope that seeds of reconciliation will take root and God's reign of peace will one day blossom.

How do we love our enemies? There are as many ways to practice *agape* toward our enemies as there are people. In recent years, Christians have begun traveling to distant lands to befriend those who suffer under U.S. militarism. Thousands of North American Christians, for example, traveled to Nicaragua during the 1980s to stand in solidarity with suffering Christians while the Reagan administration waged its brutal contra war. Hundreds journeyed to Haiti after President Aristide was overthrown by a C.I.A.-supported military coup. Some North American Christians walked through war-torn Bosnia-Hercegovnia extending the hand of nonviolent love. Many journeyed to Iraq during the 1990s, taking medical relief and opposing the U.S. Gulf war slaughter and years of brutal economic sanctions that have killed over one million people, mainly children. In 1999, I led a delegation of Nobel Peace Prize winners to Iraq to see for ourselves the effects of the U.S. economic sanctions that have killed more than one million Iraqis, mostly children under five years of age, since 1990.

But loving our enemies does not require international travel. We can stay at home, work with our local Christian community, and speak out against U.S. war-making abroad. We can call for the closing of military bases and the School of the Americas (which trains Latin American military death squads). We can demand the dismantling of our stockpile of weapons of mass destruction; assist efforts to disarm U.S.-manufactured land mines left in war zones around the world; push for cleaning up the environment polluted by nuclear weapons testing; support sister parishes and communities in Third World countries; join various peace and disarmament groups; and build a grassroots movement to abolish nuclear weapons. We can even love those who maintain our military arsenal and wear them down with our kindness, persistence, and solicitude, until they, too, accept the wisdom of nonviolence. Most importantly, we can commit the rest of our lives to this egalitarian love. Then we can trust that the Spirit of God will show us what to do.

Perhaps the most beautiful facet of Jesus' love command is its link to the nature of God. If we practice egalitarian love, Jesus says, we will become more like God. These verses offer the best description of God in all the Gospels. Unlike the imperial, vengeful, wrathful gods portrayed in the

Hebrew Scriptures, descriptions that reflect the empires' false image of God, Jesus' God showers blessings on the deserving and the undeserving alike. Love your enemies, he urges, so that "you may be children of your heavenly Father, for he makes his sun rise on the bad and the good, and causes rain to fall on the just and the unjust." If we can achieve the same egalitarian approach to humanity, we shall become God's own sons and daughters. We will become "perfect." In Jesus' eyes, we will reflect God's own love and be found faithful.

Dr. King taught that if we love our enemies instead of killing them or threatening to kill them, we will heal the world of violence. We will become God's instruments of peace. We will abolish war and the causes of war from the human heart and the face of the earth. But more importantly, we will fulfill our vocations as God's sons and daughters. That, Jesus teaches, is the most significant challenge before us: to live as God's children, to love as God loves, and to want what God wants. If we love our enemies, we make God's dream come true, and God will reign on earth as God does in heaven.

chapter seven

CONSIDER THE LILIES

"Therefore I tell you, do not worry about your life, what you will eat (or drink), or about your body, what you will wear. Is not life more than food and the body more than clothing? Look at the birds in the sky; they do not sow or reap, they gather nothing into barns, yet your heavenly Father feeds them. Are not you more important than they? Can any of you by worrying add a single moment to your life-span? Why are you anxious about clothes? Learn from the way the wild flowers grow. They do not work or spin. But I tell you that not even Solomon in all his splendor was clothed like one of them. If God so clothes the grass of the field, which grows today and is thrown into the oven tomorrow, will he not much more provide for you, O you of little faith? So do not worry and say, 'What are we to eat?' or 'What are we to drink?' or 'What are we to wear?' All these things the pagans seek. Your heavenly Father knows that you need them all. But seek first the kingdom (of God) and his righteousness, and all these things will be given you besides. Do not worry about tomorrow; tomorrow will take care of itself. (Matthew 6:25–34)

E ach year I get away for several days to a hermitage on a cliff overlooking the Atlantic Ocean on Block Island, Rhode Island. The cottage I stay in was built by the theologian William Stringfellow for Daniel Berrigan several years after Berrigan's 1970 arrest on the island for his resistance to the Vietnam War. The wild, rustic setting is both isolated and crowded by the natural world.

I write these words here, in this hermitage, on a spring morning, while robins, yellow finches, cardinals, blue jays, catbirds, blackbirds, and seagulls fly overhead. Each day Canadian geese and ringed-neck pheasants make their appearance. Recently, I saw an enormous immature bald eagle with a six-foot wingspan. The fields here are filled with gold, yellow, red, purple, and white flowers and, in some places, wild roses. Surrounded by the birds and the flowers, the ocean and the cliff, the sky and the green fields, I learn a great lesson about the providential care of our creator.

Jesus urges us to study the beauty of creation. "Notice the birds and the flowers," he tells us. "They can teach you the wisdom of the spiritual life." This beautiful passage refreshes, consoles, and recommends that we focus our priorities on what truly matters: God and God's reign. Jesus does not want us to worry about our lives. Rather, he points out the obvious: Despite all our worries and all our efforts, we cannot add a single moment to our lives. Our lifespan depends on God—so why worry? Jesus invites us to let go of our daily anxieties over food, drink, and clothing, and to seek first the reign of God and the justice of God. If we put secondary concerns in their place and set our hearts and sights on God, God's reign, and God's justice, everything we need will be given to us.

Older translations of the text use the beautiful phrase: "Consider the lilies." The word *consider* invites contemplation and calls for thoughtful reflection. Jesus wants us to ponder ordinary flowers and the lilies of the field or, in this translation, "to learn from the way the wild flowers grow." Jesus wants us to become contemplatives. "Because you have taken a close look at the natural world around you," he tells us, "you learn a basic trust in God who will provide you with the essentials you need." From this peaceful contemplation of nature, we learn to dismiss our anxieties and focus our lives on God and God's reign of justice.

This simple passage, often dismissed as pious rhetoric, is pure revolution. "Spend your lives seeking justice and the nonviolent reign of God," Jesus tells us. "Become contemplatives of God's reign, and you will be used as activists for God's reign—contemplatives-in-action for justice."

What does it mean to be a contemplative? Jesus regularly takes time alone, on a mountain or in an isolated place away from the crowd, to dwell in quiet solitude with God. In this prayerful time, his soul centers in divine peace. From this sacred space, he notices everything around him: the birds of the air, the lilies of the field, the day-to-day activities of ordinary people. Creation teaches him about the essentials of life.

Jesus wants us to be contemplatives because he wants us also to grow in wisdom. As peacemaking contemplatives in the tradition of Jesus, we, too, need to take quality time to ponder the birds of the air and the wild-flowers of the field. As we study the natural world around us, we learn the art of mindfulness and, as we grow in mindfulness, our eyes open to see the providence of God's care for creation. If we meditate on nature, we will conclude that our loving God not only cares for the creatures of the earth, but cares even more for us.

As contemplatives who meditate on natural life, we have to let go of the busyness of day-to-day life in order to concentrate on the details of creation. With time, as we concentrate on the natural beauty of our world, we come to know a freedom that liberates us from anxiety and worry. Daily meditation on creation and God's abiding presence fills us with grace, wisdom, and inner peace. As we let go of our anxieties and stop worrying about secondary nonessentials, such as food and clothing, we are free to take Jesus at his word and seek God and God's reign with our full, primary attention. As the birds, the flowers, the wind, and the ocean teach us peace, we hand over our spirits to God and become our true selves. Like the birds and the flowers, we live fully present in the moment—not anxious, not worrying. We are alive to the reality of God's abiding presence, alert to God's coming reign in our midst.

As contemplatives who have dismissed anxiety and worry from our lives, we are free to dedicate ourselves to the most important task in life. "Seek first God's reign and God's justice, and all these things will be given you besides." The will of God, the essence of life, the culmination of wisdom, is found in the pursuit of the reign of God and the justice of God. There is nothing more important. Nothing else should hold our attention. Nothing else is worth our energy, time, or effort. Here we find our purpose and discover what it means to be human.

This closing statement from the Sermon on the Mount stands as one of Jesus' great commandments. But as theologian Jim Douglass observes, it is more than a commandment: It is a natural law of the universe, as true as the law of gravity. If we drop a book, it will fall to the ground. If we seek God's reign and God's justice, everything we need in life—food, drink, clothing, everything—will be provided for us. This proverb is more than a promise; Jesus proclaims it as the natural order of life. If we seek God's reign and God's justice, the first natural result will be the daily care of our ordinary lives, including the basic necessities of food, drink, and clothing.

Having become contemplatives who let go of anxiety to focus on the reign of God, we need not worry anymore. "Do not worry about tomorrow," Jesus insists. "Focus on God. Focus on God's reign coming here and now with justice and peace for all." This primary duty sums up Christian life. This is what Jesus expects of his followers; it comprises his hope for all people.

What a liberating message: We do not have to worry anymore! We do not have to be anxious about our next meal, our drink, our clothes, and other basic needs. Even if we are poor, we can trust God to provide all the necessary things we need to live. God sends friends and community members to share with us what we need. We can ignore the anxiety caused by our culture's insistence that our lives are meaningless without its products, or that we must try to add another moment to our lives. Contemplation leads to nonviolent revolutionary activity for God's reign of justice—and, heaven knows, the culture does not want that! But the lilies do, and so do the birds, and so does Jesus.

Despite the culture's misguided insistence, we dedicate ourselves to God and God's reign because, in fact, our lives have found meaning and infinite value. They have a purpose within the entire universe. From Jesus' perspective, we have an eternal mission on which to stake our lives: to serve God, God's reign, and God's justice. We have a vocation to fulfill, and can leave its outcome and all our cares in God's hands.

As we contemplate the enormity and urgency of God's reign, our small concerns fall to the wayside; they pale in comparison. What can be greater than God's reign? What can be more important than God's justice practiced right now on earth toward all people, especially the poor and oppressed? What can be greater than doing the will of God? Nothing.

In the course of our Christian lives, a moment comes when we let go of personal ambitions and career goals, set aside childhood dreams, and take up the urgent work of proclaiming and realizing God's reign. As we respond to Jesus' call to discipleship, we seek over and over again God's reign, resist the culture's temptations, and pursue God's justice every waking moment.

The gospel liberates us from ourselves and from the culture. It frees us from the world's pointless, faithless concerns and encourages us to commit ourselves to the business of God. As contemplative workers in God's reign, we do the work that God leads us to do—and we do so without worry about the outcome or the results of our efforts on God's behalf. The reign of God belongs to God; God is in charge. God does the work and God will see to its outcome. We are merely God-seekers, doers of justice, employees of God's reign. We are focused on the present moment, today's nonviolent struggle for justice. Like the lilies and the birds, we are content to glorify God, sing God's praises, seek God's reign, and trust in God's abiding love.

As we consider the lilies and ponder the beauty of creation, we realize what our mindless violence toward the earth has done. We see how we are destroying the planet. The ozone hole has widened, the oceans are polluted, our smog destroys the air we breathe, and our nuclear weapons testing and radioactivity are literally poisoning us all. Thousands of small creatures have become extinct in recent decades because of our environmental destruction.

If we consider the lilies and the beauty of creation, we will stop destroying the earth. We will do all we can, like Jesus, to protect and heal creation.

chapter eight

THE NARROW GATE

"Enter through the narrow gate; for the gate is wide and the road broad that leads to destruction, and those who enter through it are many. How narrow the gate and constricted the road that leads to life. And those who find it are few." (Matthew 7:13–14)

The gate to destruction is wide; the gate to life is narrow. Many enter through the gate to destruction; few even find the narrow gate to life. Nonetheless, enter through the narrow gate!

Here Jesus sums up the history of the world and the doorway to salvation. The whole world gives in to destruction; few take the path to life. Yet, following the command of Deuteronomy (see 30:19–20), Jesus urges us to choose life!

What does Jesus mean by destruction? Death. What leads to massive death? War. Every country in the history of the world has organized and legalized systematic, mass murder; that is, war. The twentieth century witnessed world wars, genocidal wars, atomic blasts, concentration camps, carpet bombings, chemical attacks, and targeted missile explosions. Thousands of wars have been waged throughout history—and continue to be waged in points all over the globe at this very moment. On top of this destructive insanity, our nuclear arsenals and their radioactive toxins continue to threaten global destruction.

Why is it that most people support war? Why do people give in to the patriotic, nationalistic fervor behind militarism and support the slaughter of fellow human beings? Why do people choose destruction instead of life?

It is not just the lure of wealth that leads multinational corporations and generals to make war. It is not just the desire to the test weapons of mass destruction that we have created. It is not just the deep-seated fear we have of our opponents. Rather, we choose destruction instead of life because we are faithless. We do not believe in the living God. We do not worship the God of nonviolence, the God of peace, the God of Life. Instead, we worship the idols of death and place our faith, hope, trust, and security in our weapons. And because of this, we follow them down the wide road to destruction.

Why do so few find the narrow gate, the narrow path to life? Because it is hard to be sane when the culture around us is insane. It is hard to speak of peace in a permanent war economy. It is hard to insist on life when life is cheap, when the next war seems inevitable, when our leaders glorify the way of destruction. The few hundred conscientious objectors during World War II, for example, suffered hostility and imprisonment. The handful of Plowshares activists over the past decades who have tried to spark disarmament by hammering on nuclear silos and unarmed missiles to "beat swords into plowshares" have been ignored or dismissed by the mainstream culture and its churches; many have been viciously imprisoned. Given the trouble and persecution we invite if we oppose the culture's road to destruction, we prefer to mind our own business, make our money, pay our war taxes, submit to the culture's apathy, and not waste time struggling in "a hopeless cause" against the insurmountable imperial mindset that breeds war.

On the narrow path to life, it appears as if we are headed for destruction while on the broad road to destruction, it appears as if we are headed for life. Why is this? Because it is difficult to accept the truth that millions upon millions of us could be wrong, that we could be spiritually and politically misguided, that we could have wasted our lives insanely supporting war. It is hard to go against the crowd, indeed the majority of the human race. Because so many others glorify the nation and its militarism—from the president and government leaders to journalists and university professors to priests and rabbis—we assume that they must be right and thus convince ourselves that we are heading in the right direction.

If we do head in the opposite direction—publicly act against war and destruction, and risk persecution, arrest, imprisonment, and even death—we still may not feel like we are on the path to life. Those who speak for peace and life are often silenced and killed, like Franz Jaegerstaetter, Oscar

Romero, Jean Donovan, Ita Ford, Maura Clarke, and Dorothy Kazel. How can pain, persecution, punishment, and even death possibly be the path to life?

If we walk the way of nonviolence, we will draw the world's violence upon ourselves. As people dedicated to the God of Life, we will speak out, resist systemic violence, face the full brunt of the world's brutality, and still insist that violence and death stop here and now—in our own bodies if necessary. Indeed, in our pursuit of life, we will face death itself. But the path to life disassociates itself with the practice of death. When we refuse to retaliate with further death and destruction, the violence ceases and God's reign of nonviolence reveals itself.

Jesus shows us this dynamic in his own death. He gets killed resisting the culture's idolatry and destructive tendencies but, in the end, God raises him to new life. Although his way of nonviolence appears to lead only to pain and death, it is ultimately the path to his resurrection and eternal life.

Jesus spends his brief life walking against the on-rushing crowd, heading against the wide road to destruction, and walking the narrow path of life. For him, the narrow gate, the narrow path to life, is the way of nonviolence. He refuses to kill, to support killing, to pay for killing, to be silent in the face of killing, and to be comfortable in a world of killing. Filled with life, Jesus teaches and practices nonviolence. He possesses not a trace of destruction or violence. How does the culture of death and destruction respond to such luminous, subversive nonviolence? It labels him "possessed" and does what it only knows how to do: It kills him. But Jesus is raised to life by the God of nonviolence. His choice is affirmed—and he insists that we take that narrow path to life as well.

Jesus lives the fullest life of nonviolence. When the early community reflects on Jesus' life, death, and resurrection, they name Jesus the narrow gate. "Jesus *is* the narrow path," they say. "Jesus *is* the Way, the Truth and the Life. Jesus *is* the fullness of nonviolence." The early Christians, likewise, resist the empire's idolatrous claims and wars—and are subsequently executed, one by one. Yet, these early martyrs experience the fullness of life and, we believe, are raised up like Jesus. Their blood, mixed with the blood of Jesus, echoes through the centuries and urges us to take the same stand against war and imperial violence today. Choose life! Choose peace! Choose nonviolence! This is the message of Christ and his followers.

The narrow path of nonviolence that Jesus advocates is all encompassing; it touches every corner of our lives. Jesus calls us to a nonviolence of the heart, an inner unity and purity that reflects God's disarming love. He insists that we treat one another nonviolently on a personal level—within our families, among our friends, and in our communities. He would have us radiate peace to all those around us, throughout our ordinary day-to-day lives. He also wants us to pursue peace and nonviolence on the national and international levels as well. The gospel calls us, as Gandhi explained, to create unarmed, international peacemaking teams that will intervene and nonviolently resolve international threats and crises without weapons or war.

Jesus' nonviolence is active—and ours must be, too. "Nonviolence is not for hermits," the late United Farm Workers organizer Cesar Chavez told me. "It demands public action." The narrow path to life means engaging in the public struggle to transform structures and systems of violence into a new realm of nonviolence and justice. As Jesus teaches, when we face opposition, persecution, and suffering, we respond with peace, forgiveness, and love. Only then will our nonviolence transform others. Only then will God's reign be proclaimed and the narrow gate to life be opened.

Although our families and friends may abandon us, although we may suffer persecution and pain, although we may have to walk alone, we will find consolation in knowing that the way of nonviolence, however narrow and constricted, is the path to life. Then, as we face suffering and death, we will take heart in knowing that we have not supported the destruction of others.

William Stringfellow put it another way. In October 1968, on the evening before the trial of the Catonsville Nine, the antiwar group that burned draft records with homemade napalm, Stringfellow summed up the Christian way of life to a crowded Baltimore church:

> Remember that the State has only one power it can use against human beings: death. The State can persecute you, prosecute you, imprison you, exile you, execute you. All of these mean the same thing. The State can consign you to death. The grace of Jesus Christ in this life is that death fails. There is nothing the State can do to you, or to me, which we need fear.[1]

chapter nine

STRETCH OUT YOUR HAND

[Jesus] entered the synagogue. There was a man there who had a withered hand. They watched him closely to see if he would cure him on the sabbath so that they might accuse him. He said to the man with the withered hand, "Come up here before us." Then he said to them, "Is it lawful to do good on the sabbath rather than to do evil, to save life rather than to destroy it?" But they remained silent. Looking around at them with anger and grieved at their hardness of heart, he said to the man, "Stretch out your hand." He stretched it out and his hand was restored. The Pharisees went out and immediately took counsel with the Herodians against him to put him to death. (Mark 3:1–6)

This scene not only describes a day in the life of Jesus, but it sums up his entire life. He enters a religious sanctuary, faces the religious leaders, exposes their murderous hearts, publicly challenges their hostility, heals a poor man, and sparks such controversy that eventually the authorities execute him. The scene speaks about religious life today, our approach to the law, our willingness to heal one another, and the risks we take publicly on behalf of suffering humanity. It lifts the veil from our religious charade, pricks our passivity, and challenges us to confront injustice as Jesus did— with total disregard of the consequences.

The religious officials in the synagogue are not at all concerned about the man with the withered hand; they probably do not even notice that the man's hand is withered. They certainly would not consider healing this man's hand to be an urgent need or even a religious issue. In fact, they oppose any such activity because it is illegal. For them, following their interpretation of the law is the number-one religious duty. Any violation of the law, any threat to their control over the congregation, any public disruption of society—not to mention their sacred sanctuary—warrants excommunication and punishment. They benefit too much from their collusion with imperial and local rulers, and from repression of the poor.

These religious officials hold power over others and they intend to keep it by invoking God to legitimize their domineering authority. God's demand for justice for the poor simply is not an integral part of their worship. They do not care about healing those who suffer, and they are not concerned about the poor, except to make money off of them. They push the "unclean" to the margins of the synagogue and society, so that they themselves—the "spiritually pure"—will not be contaminated. They even scheme against anyone who threatens their control over religious life and are obsessed with catching violators of the law. Their hearts are filled not with love but violence.

Then Jesus, showing no sign of fear, walks right into their world, turns it upside-down, and confronts their hostility head-on. Calling the suffering man to come stand in the center of the sanctuary, Jesus forces the issue; he deals publicly with the man's suffering. Perhaps even the poor man would have preferred to stay out of the limelight, away from the controversy. But Jesus speaks the truth and heals the man—in total disregard of the law and the consequences of his dramatic, public action. He unmasks violence and injustice wherever he sees it, especially within the sanctuary of God. His beautiful act of healing, however, is not well received. Instead of praising God and thanking Jesus, the authorities begin to plot his murder.

One Scripture scholar calls Jesus the "great interrogator," the great questioner. If we listen carefully to the questions of Jesus, we gain greater understanding about Jesus and what he wants. When the man with the withered hand stands in the center of the sanctuary, for example, Jesus asks a gut-wrenching question that challenges the meaning of life itself: *"Is it lawful to do good on the sabbath rather than to do evil, to save life rather than to destroy it?"* (Matthew 3:4, emphasis added) Is it legal to do good or to do evil, to save life or to destroy life?

Why does Jesus talk about doing good or doing evil, saving life or destroying life, in the synagogue on the Sabbath, when everyone present is presumably actively involved in doing good and saving life? Why does he talk about engaging in evil and destruction? Why does he question the validity of the law in this setting?

Jesus sees into the hearts of those around him. He knows their allegiance lies not with God but with their strict observance of the law—which oppresses the poor. He understands the culture and the empire of his day, and he challenges those laws that dehumanize people and legalize evil. For the religious officials standing in the synagogue that day, their answer to Jesus' question is clear: It is *illegal* to do good; it is *illegal* to save life! Their law forbids any kind of disruptive activity on the Sabbath—which means that any action that threatens their tight control over the populace is outlawed. Yet, they themselves will never dare put the matter so bluntly.

Jesus breaks the law. Over and over again, throughout the Gospels, Jesus breaks every law that legalizes oppression or injustice. As far as the religious leaders are concerned, he is not law-abiding or pious or charismatic or holy. He is a troublemaking, law-breaking, disruptive, revolutionary fanatic. Because his truthfulness is so eloquent and persuasive, they fear that the people will eventually side with him. Thus, instead of learning from Jesus and following his wisdom, they look for a way to kill him.

Jesus teaches that the purpose of the Sabbath and all laws should be to do good, to save life, to heal the sick, and to serve humanity. He wants us to widen our vision and our compassion so that the life of every human being might be improved. His social analysis pinpoints how the law's control over society prevents positive social change. His question here topples our idolatry of law. When we apply his challenge to our own times, we find it questions every aspect of our culture.

Is it legal to do good or to do evil, to save life or to destroy it? The question reveals Jesus' primary concern: doing good and saving life. He is not primarily concerned with human laws, customs, rituals, traditions, religious observances, obligations, or fears. He will not stand by and watch systemic injustice oppress the poor while the religious authorities reinforce this oppression in God's name. Rather, he wants people to be healed, to show compassion to one another, to be made whole. He wants everyone, especially those assembled in God's house, to do good and save life. That is the law of life as far as Jesus is concerned.

If Jesus is willing to risk so much by confronting the systemic laws that oppress his people in God's name, imagine what he would do in our own age of genocide and nuclear weapons! He would challenge our entire social system that legalizes nuclear weapons, war, handguns, Trident submarines, air force bombers, missiles, concentration camps, bombing raids, strategic nuclear targeting, executions, and abortions. He would challenge our invoking of God's name to bless these horrors. He would challenge us as we turn our backs while the homeless freeze to death, the hungry waste away, millions live in squalor, our schools deteriorate, the environment is poisoned, prisoners are tortured, the impoverished ill are left to die, and the disenfranchised are ostracized. He would challenge our legalization of oppressing the poor and making preparations for war. On the other hand, he would applaud our nonviolent efforts to disarm our weapons, oppose executions, and challenge spending cuts that hurt the poor—actions that often lead to arrest and imprisonment. In our culture, as in Jesus' time, it still is legal to do evil and destroy life. It still is illegal to do good and save life.

"Is it lawful to do good on the sabbath rather than to do evil, to save life rather than to destroy it?" How would Jesus have us answer this question? How does he want us to live our lives? How can we heal those in our midst?

Jesus wants us to live God's law of doing good and saving life by refusing to respect any law that legalizes evil and destroys life. He wants us to live in communities of faith that heal its suffering members, for healing each other is at the heart of God's law and religious life as far as Jesus is concerned. He wants us to confront evil—actively, publicly, directly, and nonviolently—and whatever legally destroys life. He wants us to disrupt the status quo that oppresses the poor. He want us to take the same risks he took for the sake of the poor and oppressed. He wants us to call upon the poor and the oppressed to stretch out their hands in open defiance of the murderous oppressive authorities.

When Madeliene Albright appeared before a congressional committee in 1997 to be confirmed as President Clinton's secretary of state, a small handful of Christians sat in the Senate gallery. Halfway through the proceedings, several of these Christians, including a Jesuit priest from New England, stood up and, one by one, disrupted the hearings. Each person held a picture of a dying Iraqi child and called for an end to the U.S. economic sanctions against Iraq, which have killed hundreds of thousands of Iraqi children since 1990. These Christians were dragged out of the Capitol, arrested, and thrown into the D.C. central cellblock. Although a hundred reporters and press photographers, as well as leading senators and congress people, witnessed the incident, the media did not report it. Government officials were furious and dismissed their protest. When later asked about the effect of U.S. economic sanctions on the children of Iraq on the television program "60 Minutes," Albright bluntly stated that upholding U.S. interests was worth the death of the children.

Although the public action of these Christians may not have caused any immediate change in U.S. government policy toward Iraq's dying children, it faithfully followed the active Jesus who illegally healed the man with the withered hand.

As more and more Christians follow Jesus' active resistance to systemic oppression, as more and more of us publicly and dramatically confront the forces of injustice, we will be harassed, threatened, arrested, and imprisoned. But we will grow in fidelity to the compassionate Jesus and, one by one, the poor of the world will be healed.

chapter ten

THE GOOD SHEPHERD

"Whoever enters through the gate is the shepherd of the sheep. The gatekeeper opens it for him, and the sheep hear his voice, as he calls his own sheep by name and leads them out. When he has driven out all his own, he walks ahead of them, and the sheep follow him, because they recognize his voice. But they will not follow a stranger; they will run away from him, because they do not recognize the voice of strangers. . . . I am the gate for the sheep. All who came (before me) are thieves and robbers, but the sheep did not listen to them. I am the gate. Whoever enters through me will be saved, and will come in and go out and find pasture. A thief comes only to steal and slaughter and destroy; I came so that they might have life and have it more abundantly. I am the good shepherd. A good shepherd lays down his life for the sheep. A hired man, who is not a shepherd and whose sheep are not his own, sees a wolf coming and leaves the sheep and runs away, and the wolf catches and scatters them. This is because he works for pay and has no concern for the sheep. I am the good shepherd, and I know mine and mine know me, just as the Father knows me and I know the Father; and I will lay down my life for the sheep. (John 10:2–15)

Several years ago, Dorothy Sotak, my brother's mother-in-law, died suddenly on a Saturday evening after enjoying a pleasant dinner with her family. In her early sixties, Dorothy had never been sick. That night, she excused herself early saying that she wanted to lie down for a while. When her daughter checked on her a few minutes later, Dorothy was dead.

Dorothy lived a life of humble faith and loving service. When I was asked to say a few words of consolation at her funeral, I recalled the image of the Good Shepherd from John's Gospel. We are the sheep who hear his voice, who follow his direction, who go wherever he leads. "My sheep hear my voice," Jesus says. "I know them, and they follow me. I give them eternal life, and they shall never perish" (John 10:27–28). Dorothy Sotak heard the inviting voice of the Good Shepherd call her by name, I observed, and she went obediently to that better pasture: eternal life with the Good Shepherd.

The Gospels are sprinkled with the image of Jesus as the shepherd who guides his flock. Matthew, for example, writes that at the sight of the crowds, "his heart was moved with pity for them because they were troubled and abandoned, like sheep without a shepherd" (9:36). Luke relates that when the Pharisees complain because Jesus "welcomes sinners and eats with them," Jesus offers this parable:

> "What man among you having a hundred sheep and losing one of them would not leave the ninety-nine in the desert and go after the lost one until he finds it? And when he does find it, he sets it on his shoulders with great joy and, upon his arrival home, he calls together his friends and neighbors and says to them, 'Rejoice with me because I have found my lost sheep.' I tell you, in just the same way there will be more joy in heaven over one sinner who repents than over ninety-nine righteous people who have no need of repentance" (15:2, 4–7).

And when the Pharisees tell Jesus that "Herod wants to kill you," he replies, "Go and tell that fox, 'Behold, I cast out demons and I perform healings today and tomorrow, and on the third day I accomplish my purpose'" (Luke 13:31–32).

I have often wondered why Jesus does not speak more directly about Herod, Pilate, or Caesar. Perhaps the Evangelists are limited in what they can actually write because such political, critical writing would be subversive and outlawed. Perhaps Jesus focuses solely on the demonic systems of oppression, rather than the individuals who maintain them.

Although Jesus refers to Herod on only one occasion in all four Gospels, I find that this single reference answers my question. Continuing the imagery of the good shepherd, the sheep, the false shepherds, the hirelings, and the peaceful pasture of God, Jesus speaks of Herod as "that fox," as one who comes to destroy the flock. The purpose of the fox is to kill and eat the sheep. Herod the fox is the enemy of life; he and other rulers who kill and wage war, then and now, are the force of death in the world. But they are not only enemies of the flock. They are the enemies of Christ the Good Shepherd.

While steadfastly resisting the ruling authorities and their imperial reign of violence, Jesus speaks of the presences of these forces as an inevitable reality in the world. "This is the way it is," Jesus points out. "The nonviolent reign of God is coming—and is here—and we seek God's peace with all our strength, but the forces of violence, death, and destruction continue to roam through the world. Their presence cannot be denied. They must be dealt with."

Somewhere out there lurks a pack of ravenous foxes, wolves, thieves, and robbers—and their purpose is to "steal, slaughter and destroy." Thus we cannot just enjoy the pasture of life, the Gospels warn. Rather, we must protect one another from that which tries to kill us. These ruling forces that slaughter and destroy the sheep must be opposed—even if this means risking our lives. That is the story of life in the world.

The gospel assumes that we understand this reading of reality—that the imperial government and military forces will try to kill us. Jesus takes to himself the task of both the gatekeeper and the gate into God's pasture of peace, and names himself the Good Shepherd. He will lead humanity to God's pasture, protect us from the forces of death, and risk his life opposing the ruling foxes who try to kill and wage war.

The main focus of Jesus' attention, however, is not the fox, the forces of death. They are out there, of course, and they must be resisted, but he makes only one passing reference to Herod. Rather, Jesus goes to great lengths to condemn the false shepherds, those who pretend to shepherd the flock of humanity but who, in reality, do not care for the sheep and, in fact, run away when the bloodthirsty fox appears. Jesus points out that these hired shepherds are supposed to watch over and protect the sheep— that is their job—but they run away when the wolves come "because they work for pay and have no concern for the sheep" (see John 10:13).

Who are the hirelings that Jesus refers to here? According to Jesus, they are the religious leaders who pretend to care for God's people but who do not protect the flock of humanity from the forces of death. These apparently religious figures seek comfort and security and do not resist the forces of death; instead of defending the helpless flock from violence and war, they run away.

But besides the hypocritical scribes and Pharisees of the first century, John also alludes to Jesus' closest disciples and friends who "run away" at the end of the story, when the fox—the "authorities"—shows up to arrest Jesus in the Garden of Gethsemane. If we want to follow Jesus and shepherd his flock, we must plan on confronting the fox when it comes to kill the poor. Like Jesus, we will have to undergo the fox's brutal violence if we want to protect God's flock and be good and faithful shepherds.

The Evangelists draw upon this imagery from the prophets Jeremiah and Ezekiel. Jeremiah vigorously condemns the false shepherds who do not care for the flock of Israel.

> Woe to the shepherds who mislead and scatter the flock of my pasture, says the LORD. Therefore, thus says the LORD, the God of Israel, against the shepherds who shepherd my people: You have scattered my sheep and driven them away. You have not cared for them, but I will take care to punish your evil deeds. I myself will gather the remnant of my flock from all the lands to which I have driven them and bring them back to their meadow; there they shall increase and multiply. I will appoint shepherds for them who will shepherd them so that they need no longer fear and tremble; and none shall be missing, says the LORD (23:1–4).

And the prophet Ezekiel accuses the false shepherds of pasturing themselves and not God's people, the poor and oppressed:

> Woe to the shepherds of Israel who have been pasturing themselves! Should not shepherds, rather, pasture sheep? You have fed off their milk, worn their wool, and slaughtered the fatlings, but the sheep you have not pastured. You did not strengthen the weak nor heal the sick nor bind up the injured. You did not bring back the strayed nor seek the lost, but you lorded it over them harshly and brutally. So they were scattered for lack of a shepherd, and became food for all the wild beasts. My sheep were scattered and wandered over all the mountains and high hills; my sheep were scattered over the whole earth, with no one to look after them or to search for them.
>
> Therefore, shepherds, hear the word of the LORD: As I live, says the Lord GOD, because my sheep have been given over to pillage, and because my sheep have become food for every wild beast, for lack of a shepherd; because my shepherds did not look after my sheep, but

pastured themselves and did not pasture my sheep; because of this, shepherds, hear the word of the LORD: Thus says the Lord GOD: I swear I am coming against these shepherds. I will claim my sheep from them and put a stop to their shepherding my sheep so that they may no longer pasture themselves. I will save my sheep, that they may no longer be food for their mouths.

For thus says the Lord GOD: I myself will look after and tend my sheep. As a shepherd tends his flock when he finds himself among his scattered sheep, so will I tend my sheep. I will rescue them from every place where they were scattered when it was cloudy and dark. I will lead them out from among the peoples and gather them from the foreign lands; I will bring them back to their own country and pasture them upon the mountains of Israel (in the land's ravines and all its inhabited places). In good pastures will I pasture them, and on the mountain heights of Israel shall be their grazing ground . . . I myself will pasture my sheep; I myself will give them rest, says the Lord GOD. The lost I will seek out, the strayed I will bring back, the injured I will bind up, the sick I will heal (but the sleek and the strong I will destroy), shepherding them rightly . . . I will save my sheep so that they may no longer be despoiled, and I will judge between one sheep and another. I will appoint one shepherd over them to pasture them . . . I will make a covenant of peace with them, and rid the country of ravenous beasts, that they may dwell securely in the desert and sleep in the forests (34:2–16, 22–23, 25).

Jeremiah, Ezekiel, and Jesus rail against those who pretend to shepherd the flock of humanity but who, in reality, are interested in only their own comfort and job security. The prophets seek true shepherds who speak out for the defenseless, rescue the poor, and risk their lives to protect others from the forces of violence. Jesus, of course, fulfills the prophets' vision and becomes God's "covenant of peace" who is ridding the world of violence. Jesus the Good Shepherd risks his life for the flock of humanity so that we might all be one in God's nonviolent pasture of peace.

John's Gospel as well as the Book of Revelation, however, carry this image even further. The Good Shepherd becomes the Lamb of God slaughtered and sacrificed for the flock. Then, after his resurrection, the Good Shepherd, the Lamb of God, invites Peter and all disciples to feed his sheep and tend his lambs. We, the sheep, hearing his voice, are then called to become good shepherds who protect the flock and lead it into God's pasture. After feeding Christ's sheep and tending his lambs, we, like Peter, are called to follow the Good Shepherd on the way of the cross. We are to become, like Christ, lambs sacrificed for God's reign of justice and peace in God's redemptive struggle against the fox's forces of death.

The New Testament proclaims that the risen Jesus continues to shepherd the flock of humanity, and Christians today pray Psalm 23 to Christ as they follow him into God's pasture of peace:

> The LORD is my shepherd,
>> there is nothing I lack.
> In green pastures you let me graze;
>> to safe waters you lead me;
>> you restore my strength.
> You guide me along the right path
>> for the sake of your name.
> Even when I walk through a dark valley,
>> I fear no harm for you are at my side;
>> your rod and staff give me courage . . .
> Only goodness and love will pursue me
>> all the days of my life;
> I will dwell in the house of the LORD
>> for years to come (1–4, 6).

Likewise, Isaiah describes the nonviolent messiah as "a shepherd [who] feeds his flock, . . . [who] gathers the lambs" (40:11).

The image of the Good Shepherd was central to the pastoral life of Salvadoran Archbishop Oscar Romero, assassinated while offering Eucharist on March 24, 1980. One month before he was killed by the military, he traveled to Belgium to receive an honorary degree from the University of Louvain. In his speech he explained:

> I am a shepherd who, with his people, has begun to learn a beautiful and difficult truth: our Christian faith requires that we submerge ourselves in this world. The world that the church must serve is the world of the poor, and the poor are the ones who decide what it means for the church to really live in the world. It is the poor who force us to understand what is really taking place. The persecution of the church is a result of defending the poor. Our persecution is nothing more nor less than sharing in the destiny of the poor.[1]

66

Back in El Salvador a few days later, Romero told a reporter:

> My life has been threatened many times. I have to confess that as a Christian, I don't believe in death without resurrection. If they kill me, I will rise again in the Salvadoran people. As a shepherd I am obliged by divine law to give my life for those I love, for the Salvadoran people, including those Salvadorans who threaten to assassinate me. If they should go so far as to carry out their threats, I want you to know that I offer my blood to God for justice and the resurrection of El Salvador.[2]

Romero's life and death gives us a striking modern-day example of following and emulating the Good Shepherd. Like Romero and all the saints and martyrs, we too will one day hear the Good Shepherd's voice and be welcomed into the pasture of peace, where there are no more foxes, no more wolves, no more violence, and no more wars.

But because his flock of sheep still needs protection from the foxes of war and the wolves of violence, Christ bids us to become good shepherds and nonviolent lambs who give their lives for the flock of humanity. We accept this invitation with confidence because he leads us, he knows our names, we know his voice and, one day, we trust, he will lead us, too, into his pasture of peace.

chapter eleven

GIVE THEM SOME FOOD

[Jesus] received [the crowd] and spoke to them about the kingdom of God, and he healed those who needed to be cured. As the day was draw-ing to a close, the Twelve approached him and said, "Dismiss the crowd so that they can go to the surrounding villages and farms and find lodg-ing and provisions; for we are in a deserted place here." He said to them, "Give them some food yourselves." They replied, "Five loaves and two fish are all we have, unless we ourselves go and buy food for all these people." Now the men there numbered about five thousand. Then he said to his disciples, "Have them sit down in groups of (about) fifty." They did so and made them all sit down. Then taking the five loaves and the two fish, and looking up to heaven, he said the blessing over them, broke them, and gave them to the disciples to set before the crowd. They all ate and were satisfied. And when the leftover fragments were picked up, they filled twelve wicker baskets. (Luke 9:11–17)

Jesus attracts crowds of people wherever he goes. He captivates them with his reflections on God's reign of peace and heals those in need. Toward the end of one particular day, his friends urge him to tell the crowd to go home so that they can get something to eat, "for we are in a deserted place here." Perhaps his friends are hungry and want some food them-selves—or maybe they are just plain tired. Whenever we read that people are in a deserted place, however, we know something significant will occur, for the Gospels insist that God actively works on the margins of society in deserted places.

Jesus responds by telling the disciples to do something themselves for the people. He issues one of the great commands of the Scriptures: "Give them some food yourselves." But the disciples protest: "That's crazy! We have only a little food, and you want us to feed this huge crowd? We barely have enough for ourselves. Do you want us to go and buy food for all these people?"

Jesus will hear none of it. (In typical patriarchal fashion, the Evangelist notes that the crowd numbered "about five thousand men." Matthew 14:13–21 adds: "Not counting women and children.") Jesus tells the disciples to have the crowd sit down in small groups of about fifty, thus forming small communities that are more manageable, more human. As small groups of people gather together, the "crowd" actually disappears and individual people begin to stand out. Each person becomes a significant member of the smaller group, not a statistic lost in the crowd.

The people have been standing, probably close against one another, for a good part of the day. When they finally sit down in groups, they spread out, relax, stretch, rest, and get to know one another. Once these small communities are formed, once everyone is seated, once people have introduced themselves, Jesus takes the food, looks up to heaven, blesses the food, breaks the food, and gives the food to the disciples "to set before the crowd." The crowd, of course, watches what Jesus is doing; they see the food that is set out before them, and they understand that Jesus is sharing the little food he has with his own small community. Inspired by this beautiful act of generosity and the spiritual, loving atmosphere Jesus has created with his words about God's reign, the people begin to do likewise. They recognize that Jesus and his friends are having a picnic—and they do the same. As they take out the little food they have, look to heaven, bless their food, break it, and share it with one another, the air is filled with celebration. (One surmises that the women and children, not included in the estimation of the crowd's size, actually begin this imitation of Jesus. One can also surmise that they are the first to share their food with one another, unlike the male disciples who cannot conceive of a picnic in such a deserted place with such a large crowd.)

When people share their food with one another in small interpersonal communities, everyone gets enough to eat—and there is food left over. The miracle is that, instead of hording their food for themselves (as the male disciples recommend), people follow Jesus' example and share what little food they have.

The Gospels portray this sharing of food as a religious act of God. The people look to heaven, bless their food, break it (that is, split it up for the purpose of sharing it with others), and give it to one another. In this way, everyone is fed; everyone is filled; everyone is comfortable and relaxed in the presence of Jesus. After his all-day retreat on the reign of God, this experience literally offers a foretaste of God's reign.

This miracle is one of the few events, along with Jesus' action in the Temple and his crucifixion, recorded in all four Gospels (see Matthew 14:13–21; Mark 6:30–44; John 6:1–14). It portrays the Eucharist in human terms and demonstrates its social justice implications. It invites us to break out of our ordinary mindset to reach out to those around us, even to the point of sharing our food with others. Jesus commands us to a just economic redistribution of our food—to feed the hungry—a command that should push the churches to end world hunger.

Jesus also summons us to be human with one another by forming small communities, where relating is more personal. Once this happens, the barriers between individuals melt away and we rediscover the human bonds that connect us to one another. We befriend one another and, in the light of prayer and grace, in the aura of Jesus' words about God's reign, we find ourselves wanting to share what we have. We want to celebrate the presence of Jesus in our midst by joining him in a picnic celebration.

Jesus is the one who brings us together, who teaches us about God's reign, who heals our brokenness, who invites us to form community, and who shows us how to share our food and our lives with others. He knows that we easily get lost in a crowd, that in our individualistic world we are determined to survive the crowd, mind our own business, take care of ourselves, and step over others if necessary. But with that selfish attitude, we never break out of the crowd. Only by forming community with others, as Jesus commands, will we become human with others. Then the crowd will dissolve and new friendships will emerge. We will celebrate and share together the Lord's Eucharist.

Through a literalist interpretation, we can easily dismiss this story as something that happened only once, a long time ago, when Jesus walked the earth. But if we try to experience the story today, by joining a small community of faith and sharing our food and resources with others, we discover that not only is there plenty of food to go around, but the hostile faces in the crowd around us have been transformed. Suddenly we have new friends with whom to share our faith and our lives.

This miracle story is more than a demand for economic justice; it goes beyond the mandate to feed the starving peoples of the earth. This miracle invites us to friendship and relationship with one another. Not only do we take care of one another, feed one another, shelter one another, and heal one another, but we welcome each other into our own communal circle of friends and discover our common humanity. When we do this, we discover not only our best human selves but also Christ in our midst. This story gives a vivid portrait of God's reign in heaven as an eternal banquet with Jesus in the center. If we dare to share our food, our hearts, our faith, and our lives with one another in community, we will experience Christ in our midst and taste the reign of God.

chapter twelve

INVITE THE POOR

He said to the host who invited him, "When you hold a lunch or a din-
ner, do not invite your friends or your brothers or your relatives or your
wealthy neighbors, in case they may invite you back and you have repay-
ment. Rather, when you hold a banquet, invite the poor, the crippled, the
lame, the blind; blessed indeed will you be because of their inability to
repay you. For you will be repaid at the resurrection of the righteous."
(Luke 14:12–14)

Jesus loves great feasts, good food, fine wine, and celebrations. In fact,
one gets the impression that his short life is filled with parties. While he
daily faces the forces of death and deliberately heads down the road of
resistance to a sure execution, he loves life and lives it to the full. He enjoys
his evening meals with those he meets on his journey, and makes sure that
his joy is shared with outcasts.

In these frequently recurring gospel scenes, are we being told something about Jesus' own personality? Is Jesus amiably, sociably, and
continuously making new friends? Are the Evangelists telling us that Jesus
is not only a nonviolent revolutionary but a delight to be with? When we
read between the lines we can grasp what a scandal he is. Luke repeatedly
notes that the religious leaders are appalled at his behavior. "[He] welcomes sinners and eats with them" (Matthew 11:19), the religious leaders
comment in shock (see Luke 15:2). "He is a glutton and a drunkard," they
complain. Indeed, Jesus and his followers are portrayed as a wandering
band of ne'er-do-wells, with Jesus as the life of the party.

A dinner with Jesus is an occasion of joy. In keeping with the spirit of
Judaism, Jesus turns a meal into a ritual of friendship, faith-sharing, and
communion. A meal with Jesus is also an experience of God's abiding

presence. Jesus welcomes those he meets and shares meals with them. He encourages feasting and drinking, tells stories and parables, and transforms meals into intimate sharings of faith and hope.

But that is not all. The Gospels tell us that Jesus consistently makes a preferential option for the poor. If he loves to feast at table, he wants the feasts to include those most in need, those pushed to society's margins. Jesus offers his life to the poor, the crippled, the lame, the blind, and the outcast. He wants them to enjoy life, so it is only fitting that he welcome them at table with him. John's Gospel testifies that this is his mission, "that they may have life and life to the full" (see 10:10).

When Jesus tells his host to invite the poor to parties, he isn't being a rude, ungrateful guest. Rather, he is revealing the secret of life, a way to share God's blessings. "You like to give parties," he tells the host. "You can afford to give parties," he observes. "Then keep on giving dinner parties— only be sure you invite the poor and the marginalized who are unable to repay you. You not only will discover great joy and meaning in your life, but you will receive the blessing of God."

For Jesus, unconditional service toward those who are incapable of repayment is a key to life's blessings. Throwing parties for the poor and the outcast is not a burdensome duty; rather, Jesus wants us to celebrate. He wants us to serve lunch and dinner parties and feasts. But he wants our lunches and dinner parties and feasts to be centered explicitly on those who are poor, crippled, lame, and blind: those who cannot repay us!

Jesus recommends that we do what he himself does when he feeds the five thousand: He feeds the crowd without any possibility that they can repay him. He is typically selfless in his giving, and he wants others to adopt his large-hearted generosity. He must have felt joy in his heart as he fed those in need, served those who could not repay him, and offered parties for those who suffered. He wants to share with others the blessing he has received from all those who are unable to repay him. He wants us to get beyond ourselves, to see beyond our immediate circle, to offer "senseless acts of generosity" to those who are incapable of repaying. When we serve those who cannot repay us, we will be repaid by God on the day of resurrection.

Jesus' advice is simple, yet few of us have the courage to put his message into practice. Hospitality to the poor has drifted away from our daily faith life. Today, not unlike Jesus' day, we throw parties for our friends, relatives, and wealthy neighbors—and forget the plight of the poor. At best, we make charitable contributions to those who serve the poor. All the while, the culture continues to crush the poor by cutting welfare assistance, allowing people to starve, permitting the homeless to suffer on the streets, and raising the price of decent healthcare. The culture does not place the poor at the center of its concern; rather, the culture caters to the wealthy.

Thus Jesus is counter-cultural, even a-cultural; he wants us to put the poor and the marginalized at the center of our ordinary lives, as the focus of our lunch and dinner parties. If the meal is the most profound, intimate part of Jewish life in Jesus' day, then his command to "invite the poor" asks us to welcome the poor into the most intimate place of our lives: our table fellowship.

In 1932, Dorothy Day and Peter Maurin took up Jesus' advice by welcoming the homeless to their kitchen table and opening the first Catholic Worker house of hospitality. In the early 1960s, Jean Vanier accepted Jesus' advice and welcomed two handicapped men into his home in France and began the worldwide L'Arche movement, a network of community homes for the crippled, the lame, the blind, the handicapped, and their assistants. Today, L'Arche houses continue to celebrate life at every opportunity with their "core" community members. They have created havens of joy for those in pain. In the early 1980s, two professors of Russian literature at New York University began to discuss the growing homelessness in their Lower East Side neighborhood. They approached Nativity Church, a neighborhood Jesuit parish, and arranged to serve a weekly meal to the poor and the homeless in the church hall. Instead of standard soup-kitchen fare, they offered a restaurant atmosphere with beautifully decorated tables. All the food and supplies were donated, and volunteers seated the "guests" and served each table personally. For nearly fifteen years, their "free restaurant" has served an excellent meal in an atmosphere of peace to those most in need. Every Saturday for two years in the mid-1980s, I helped serve the meal. Each day was a blessing not only for those who enjoyed the free meal, but for those of us who served it as well.

The Sacred Heart Center in Richmond, Virginia, is another rare place that practices the Gospel's command to party with those unable to offer repayment. With over thirty people on staff (a third of them low-income, African-American women from the neighborhood), this community center offers licensed day care, after-school care, and summer programs for children; a family literacy program (with academic training and parenting skills for women); a program for teens; jobs for residents; emergency fuel and food assistance; kindergarten, first and second grade classes for at-risk children; parent support groups; a healthcare program; and a recreation program for over 250 men. In addition to this ambitious list of services, the center also hosts various community-wide events and activities. This center was founded by the Jesuits and the local Catholic diocese, and I feel fortunate for having been privileged to serve as its director for two years (1995–1996).

Our neighborhood was not only the poorest, most violent, and most marginalized in the city of Richmond, but in the entire state of Virginia— and it held the second highest murder rate in the country. Yet, the center is bursting with life. One Thanksgiving, for example, we threw a party for the neighborhood. Our benefactors and friends baked a delicious smorgasbord that filled four long, decorated tables. As the children, teens, and mothers from low-income neighborhood families entered our gym, their eyes bulged and their mouths salivated. We gathered in a great circle in our gym and together—young children, teens, moms, the elderly, the lame, the crippled, volunteers, staff, and friends of the center—joined hands, bowed their heads, and gave thanks to God for all the blessings of life. Then we sat down together for the banquet. What a joyful celebration! That day we felt so blessed by God that I thought we caught a foretaste of the heavenly banquet. Then, shortly before Christmas, we celebrated another feast with the children and their mothers, gave away dozens of turkeys with all the fixings, and distributed over 1400 individually wrapped gifts to neighborhood children and families. We were blessed in these efforts and had a good time as well.

Jesus certainly wants us to resist the forces of death, but there is no question that he also wants us to celebrate life. If we can afford to have lunch and dinner parties, then by all means, he insists, invite those who cannot offer repayment. Together you will enjoy a foretaste of the heavenly banquet. In this way your lives will not only serve the poor and marginalized, but they will be filled with celebration.

chapter thirteen

NEITHER DO I CONDEMN YOU

Early in the morning [Jesus] arrived again in the temple area, and all the people started coming to him, and he sat down and taught them. Then the scribes and the Pharisees brought a woman who had been caught in adultery and made her stand in the middle. They said to him, "Teacher, this woman was caught in the very act of committing adultery. Now in the law, Moses commanded us to stone such women. So what do you say?" They said this to test him, so that they could have some charge to bring against him. Jesus bent down and began to write on the ground with his finger. But when they continued asking him, he straightened up and said to them, "Let the one among you who is without sin be the first to throw a stone at her." Again he bent down and wrote on the ground. And in response, they went away one by one, beginning with the elders. So he was left alone with the woman before him. Then Jesus straightened up and said to her, "Woman, where are they? Has no one condemned you?" She replied, "No one, sir." Then Jesus said, "Neither do I condemn you. Go, (and) from now on do not sin anymore." (John 8:2–11)

This scene sums up the gospel, Jesus' life message, and the world's crisis: the choice between violence or nonviolence, murder or mercy, condemnation or compassion, revenge or reconciliation, death or life. Much to the dismay and resentment of the scribes and the Pharisees, Jesus is teaching in the Temple and is attracting the attention of a great crowd. In an attempt to catch Jesus in theological heresy, the authorities bring him a woman and stand her in the middle of the crowd in front of him. They want to put to death not only the woman but Jesus as well.

As tension fills the air, we notice that the man who committed adultery with this woman is not being charged. In these patriarchal days, women are not considered fully human by men, especially religious men. Women are blamed by men for the problems of men. Capital punishment is the solution to most crimes, including the crime of adultery. Although the Romans legally crucify troublemakers, the religious authorities sanction stoning lawbreakers to death. These men have the legal support to condemn this woman to death—right here in the Temple, the holiest ground in the Judaic world—and then to stone her to death themselves.

With ideological, patriarchal venom dripping from their mouths, and jealousy and murder raging in their hearts, the religious authorities question Jesus: "In the law Moses commanded us to stone such women. So what do you say?" They resemble those who resisted Jesus in the Galilee synagogue where he healed the man with the withered hand.

As they push Jesus to join their rage and support their murderous intent, they must be shocked to see Jesus bend down and write on the ground. They stand ready to commit murder, and Jesus responds by bending down and writing on the ground, as if ignoring their question.

I have long believed that Jesus was the most disarming presence the world has ever known. His spiritual peace and love must have touched the hearts of others very deeply. Over the centuries, we have glimpsed his disarming power in spiritual figures like Francis of Assisi, Gandhi, and Mother Teresa. The very act of bending down and writing on the ground in the face of a hostile mob literally draws attention away from anger to what he is writing. The crowd must have thought: "What is he doing? Doesn't he hear us? Doesn't he know that we are about to kill this sinful woman? Why doesn't he answer us?"

Jesus' slow, patient, quiet, non-response opens a space for the religious authorities to hear his answer. If he had shouted at them or engaged them in theological argument, they probably would have stoned the woman then and there in a burst of rage. Instead, his quiet drawing on the ground begins the process of disarmament. It changes the focus of attention from their righteous indignation to his scribbling on the ground. It sets the stage so that they can hear his answer and let it sink down through their anger to the depths of their own sinful hearts. Once they get beyond their own intent—to catch Jesus breaking the law and try to figure out what he is doing on the ground—they are ready to hear his answer. Then, when he knows he has their attention, Jesus stands up and issues one of the greatest of all commandments: "Let the one without sin cast the first stone."

In a sentence, Jesus not only condemns the death penalty but he points out the sinfulness within each one of us. His piercing truth disarms us of our intent to murder others in acts of righteous revenge. Jesus' words shock the scribes and Pharisees, of course, beginning with the elders, who realize their own violence, sinfulness, and complicity. They know they have broken the Mosaic law by looking upon the couple in the first place. (According to Mosaic law, the one who witnesses the act of adultery is also guilty of violating the law and can be condemned.) One by one, they walk away and, suddenly, the Temple is empty and Jesus stands alone with the woman.

What a contrast to the opening description of the adoring students. No more crowds; no more religious leaders; no more attentive listeners; perhaps no more disciples! The accusers recognize their sinfulness in the presence of Jesus and walk away from their intent to kill the woman.

But the amazing story does not end here. Jesus goes on to engage the woman in dialogue. Such an exchange alone would have infuriated the self-righteous religious leaders. And even though the answer is obvious, Jesus asks the woman what happened:

> "Woman, where are they? Has no one condemned you?" She replied, "No one, sir." Then Jesus said, "Neither do I condemn you. Go, (and) from now on do not sin anymore" (John 10:10–11).

"Neither do I condemn you." These beautiful words betray the culture's inaccurate portrait of God as a vengeful God. Here we witness the mercy, compassion, and nonviolence of Jesus, who does not condemn. In resisting death and disarming the theologians, the fundamentalists, and the would-be executioners, Jesus saves the condemned. Indeed, he becomes the condemned one himself, and thus redeems us. In this way he reveals that God is a God of mercy, compassion, and clemency.

Even if Jesus had not been crucified legally—a victim of the death penalty—this story instructs Christians that they cannot support the death penalty. If we want to follow Jesus, we have to stop bringing others into the center of public controversy for revenge and execution; we must stop condemning others to death, even if they appear to "deserve" death because of their crime.

The great command, "Let the one without sin be the first to throw a stone," could be translated in a variety of ways: Let the one without sin be the first to throw the switch on the electric chair. Let the one without sin be the first to inject deadly poison into the arm of another human being. Let the one without sin be the first to hang another. Let the one without sin be the first to raise a machete and hack one's tribal enemy to death. Let the one without sin be the first to pull the trigger of a handgun and kill one's religious enemy or one's assailant or someone who has caused pain. Let the one without sin be the first to abort an unborn child. Let the one without sin be the first to push a button and fire a missile. Let the one without sin be the first to throw the switch and drop a nuclear bomb.

There is not one of us who is without sin; we are all sinners. In the depths of our hearts, we are all guilty of the worst crimes of violence. From Jesus' perspective, from God's perspective, each one of us has chosen violence and death deep within. We have all stood in complicity with mass murder, war, nuclear destruction, the environment's degradation, the genocide of starvation, executions, abortion, and oppression. We are all guilty of adultery and murder in our hearts, as Jesus explains in the Sermon on the Mount. Not one of us has the right to throw a stone and kill another because not one of us is without sin, including murderous violence, in our hearts. We all have felt in our hearts the desire to throw a stone at another and, as far as Jesus is concerned, our common sinfulness invalidates any righteousness or justification that we might claim. As the psalmists and prophets observe, we are all wicked in God's sight.

Jesus wants us to live in the truth of our sinfulness before God so that we might turn to God for mercy and learn to be merciful to one another. As we begin to practice mercy and nonviolence toward one another, we enter into the mercy of God. As we refuse to condemn others, God refuses to condemn us. As we grant clemency to others, God grants clemency to us. As we practice nonviolence with one another, God rejoices that we are at last becoming the faithful people of nonviolence that God calls us to be.

This spiritual law of mercy is at the heart of Jesus' message. Luke sums up his account of Jesus' Sermon on the Plain with this command:

> "Be merciful, just as (also) your Father is merciful. Stop judging and you will not be judged. Stop condemning and you will not be

condemned. Forgive and you will be forgiven. Give and gifts will be given to you; a good measure, packed together, shaken down, and overflowing, will be poured into your lap" (Luke 6:36–38).

As the spirit of vengeance and violence spreads across the nation, we need to center ourselves in this fundamental gospel teaching. I recall when Timothy McVeigh was convicted for blowing up the Oklahoma City Federal Building, murdering over one hundred people. While news commentators, politicians, victims' family members, government officials, and ordinary churchgoers called for his execution, I found myself wondering how Jesus would respond to McVeigh's crime. What would Jesus do?

The gospel gives us the answer: "Let the one without sin be the first to cast a stone." We are not allowed to kill. We are not allowed to execute anyone. As followers of Jesus, we oppose the death penalty. We practice compassion, forgiveness, mercy, and reconciliation—even toward those who kill our loved ones or ourselves. We refuse to condemn anyone to death. Like Jesus, we grant clemency to everyone and, in the process, we dwell in the clemency of God.

chapter fourteen

WALKING ON WATER

[Jesus] made the disciples get into the boat and precede him to the other side, while he dismissed the crowds. After doing so, he went up on the mountain by himself to pray. When it was evening he was there alone. Meanwhile the boat, already a few miles offshore, was being tossed about by the waves, for the wind was against it. During the fourth watch of the night, he came toward them, walking on the sea. When the disciples saw him walking on the sea they were terrified. "It is a ghost," they said, and they cried out in fear. At once (Jesus) spoke to them, "Take courage, it is I; do not be afraid." Peter said to him in reply, "Lord, if it is you, command me to come to you on the water." He said, "Come." Peter got out of the boat and began to walk on the water toward Jesus. But when he saw how (strong) the wind was he became frightened; and, beginning to sink, he cried out, "Lord, save me!" Immediately Jesus stretched out his hand and caught him, and said to him, "O you of little faith, why did you doubt?" After they got into the boat, the wind died down. Those who were in the boat did him homage, saying, "Truly, you are the Son of God." (Matthew 14:22–33.)

What was it like to walk through the Galilean countryside with Jesus? The Gospels offer a glimpse of his compassion, his sincere interest in everyone, his wisdom, his gentleness, his wit, his courage. Yet, these descriptions only scratch the surface. Throughout their testimonies, the Evangelists take pains to portray Jesus' daring deeds. He does the impossible: He travels to enemy territory and converses with the enemy as if he loves them. In fact, he does love them. In fact, he heals and liberates his enemies. He is bold and provocative, and he expects his followers to do as he does; he wants them to risk their lives, to reconcile everyone, and to radiate the truth of nonviolence. He urges them to go "to the other side," to meet their culture's enemies, and to carry forth the good news of God's reconciling love. He believes they will do greater works than he.

In an effort to describe Jesus' dramatic nonviolence, three of the Evangelists tell the fantastic tale of Jesus walking on water. Perhaps his extraordinary journey to the other side, to the land of the enemy, could be explained in no other way. Matthew's account begins with Jesus deliberately sending the disciples ahead without him, out onto the sea, to the other side, to Gentile territory. Jesus then ascends a mountain alone for a night of prayer. The disciples had probably never been to the other side of the Sea of Galilee and knew only animosity toward Gentiles and Samaritans, their enemies. Immediately, a storm rises, and they are tossed about by the waves while a harsh wind bears down upon them. The storm symbolizes their fear and inner turmoil over the journey to the other side, to the land of the enemy.

Suddenly Jesus appears to them walking on water—and they are terrified. Thinking it is a ghost, they cry out with fear, we are told a second time. The disciples are tossed about by the storm and fear for their lives. Jesus, on the other hand, walks calmly on the water, peacefully to the other side, right through the storm. His nonviolence is fearless, flawless, and faith-filled. "Take courage, it is I; do not be afraid," Jesus tells them. "Lord, if it is you," Peter shouts back, "Command me to come to you on the water." "Come," Jesus tells Peter.

Keeping his eyes on Jesus, Peter steps out of the boat and begins to walk on the water toward Jesus. But the moment he takes his eyes off Jesus to look down at the water, he sees how strong the wind is, becomes frightened, and begins to sink.

"Lord, save me!" Peter cries out.

Immediately Jesus stretches out his hand and catches Peter. "O you of little faith, why did you doubt?" he asks.

Once they are back in the boat, the wind dies down and, for the first time in the saga of Jesus, the disciples offer him homage, saying, "Truly, you are the Son of God."

Have we ever traveled to enemy territory? Have we ever faced the fear of entering a war zone and conversing with the enemy about peace? Have we, like Peter, ever been invited to walk the stormy waters of reconciliation?

Have we ever nearly drowned from fear because of our peacemaking efforts, only to be pulled from the water and saved by God at the last minute? When we meditate on the dramatic deeds of the faithful figures of our times—people like Rosa Parks, Cesar Chavez, Oscar Romero, and Edith Stein—we realize that at times they felt like they were at sea in a storm, that they saw a ghost walking on water, that the Lord called them to walk on water, and that the Lord pulled them up as they lost confidence and sank.

The image of walking on water describes the risky, political work of nonviolence and social reconciliation. Indeed, as we see from the lives of these noble peacemakers, walking on water seems easier than making peace and seeking justice. Which is easier, for example, to dismantle nuclear weapons, end capital punishment, outlaw war, end world hunger, heal disease—or walk on water?

Before Maryknoll sister Ita Ford was killed, along with three other churchwomen in El Salvador on December 2, 1980, she spent many years working among the poor in Chile with another Maryknoll sister, her close friend, Carla Piette. They both moved to El Salvador shortly after Archbishop Oscar Romero's assassination in March 1980. A few months later, they began to work among the poor in the war-torn northern province of Chalatenango. In August, while Ita and Carla were driving a priest and several *campesinos*, their jeep was caught in a flash flood and was flipped over onto the driver's side. Carla was trapped but managed to push Ita through the window. Once free of the vehicle, Ita was swept down the flooding river until she managed to catch hold of a bush and survive. Fearing that she was about to drown, Ita kept repeating, "Receive me Lord, I'm coming." Ita survived, and the next day, Jean Donovan, the young missioner, found Carla's body fourteen kilometers down stream.

A week before she died, Carla wrote to another Maryknoll sister about her work and her struggles:

> Civil war is messy, no doubt about that. It's also frustrating when one works for the Church and God who is for people and not for this side or that. At present I am chauffeuring a young priest who has been threatened. I drive food to different places, talk with different people, carry on and on with the Lord about what is happening with this valiant *pueblo*. The Salvadorans are sharp and strong and have nerves

of steel. In one place in the *campo* in the middle of Mass when the shooting started, the women just got up, looked around and knelt down, the men closed the doors, and the priest whom I drive just stood and waited and then continued Mass. No hysteria, no leaving the church, just a bit of commotion as Carla sits on the bench and looks around and says inside, "What have I come to?" It's a barrel of laughs—especially as the priest whom I chauffeur says, "Step on the gas!" over roads that even Toyota ads wouldn't come near to describing. So, the walk continues and the Lord of the Way leads each day with no map and no clear weather, but rather fog and total trust. But after it all—like Peter, I'm glad I jumped out of the boat and said, "If it's you, Lord, bid me come," and He says, "Come." So I dolly on the waves, sinking, screaming out, but holding His hand. I know He's here and I'm glad I am.[1]

Like the four women martyrs who died four months later, Carla obeyed Christ, journeyed to the other side, walked on water, loved the enemies of her country, and practiced nonviolence. She truly worshiped the nonviolent Christ.

What would it be like for us to do likewise? It would be like Catholics and Protestants in Northern Ireland reconciling with one another, seeking peace together, and nonviolently non-cooperating with imperial domination. It would be like Muslims and Christians in the former Yugoslavia renouncing their violence, letting go of past grievances, forgiving one another, seeking reconciliation, and building a new society based on justice for everyone. It would be like wealthy, white, North American suburbanites journeying into the cities, renouncing their somnolent isolation, reaching out to low-income families, breaking down the barriers of racism and classism, befriending new sisters and brothers, housing the homeless, rebuilding schools, supporting youth, and sharing their wealth. Such actions would be risky; they would court persecution, rejection, violence, and death. Yet, they would proclaim God's reign here and now in our divided world.

At some point in our lives, Jesus tells each of us to get in the boat and go to the other side, to enemy territory. Along the way, we face the frightening storms that rise from the work of nonviolence and reconciliation. Yet, as we embark on this stormy mission, we see Jesus calmly walk toward us on the water. We hear his call, step out of the boat, walk out onto the water, start to sink, and get saved by his strong arm. This miraculous drama sums up the gospel journey of life. With Jesus' help, we know we need not fear. We can ride those waves, survive the storm, and carry on the peacemaking mission of reconciliation and love for our enemies. We can make it safely to the other side. Like Carla, we will be grateful to be at the side of our peacemaking Lord.

chapter fifteen

WHO DO YOU SAY THAT I AM?

Along the way [Jesus] asked his disciples, "Who do people say that I am?"
They said in reply, "John the Baptist, others Elijah, still others one of the
prophets." And he asked them, "But who do you say that I am?" Peter
said to him in reply, "You are the Messiah." Then he warned them not to
tell anyone about him.

He began to teach them that the Son of Man must suffer greatly and
be rejected by the elders, the chief priests, and the scribes, and be killed,
and rise after three days. He spoke this openly. Then Peter took him aside
and began to rebuke him. At this he turned around and, looking at his
disciples, rebuked Peter and said, "Get behind me, Satan. You are think-
ing not as God does, but as human beings do."

He summoned the crowd with his disciples and said to them, "Who-
ever wishes to come after me must deny himself [or herself], take up [their]
cross, and follow me. For whoever wishes to save his [or her] life will lose
it, but whoever loses his [or her] life for my sake and that of the gospel
will save it. What profit is there for one to gain the whole world and
forfeit his [or her] life? What could one give in exchange for his[or her]
life?" (Mark 8:27–37)

Jesus' questions get right to the heart of reality. His greatest question
marks a turning point in the Synoptic Gospels: "Who do people say
that I am?" Is he trying to find out if his message is understood—or does a
deeper search lie behind the question? The disciples offer various responses:
John the Baptist, Elijah, one of the prophets. *"But who do you say that I*
am?" he asks them.

This is a question to ponder for the rest of our lives. *"Who do you say*
that I am?" Jesus wants his disciples to know who he is, but he wants them
to discover that for themselves. He wants to hear it from them—and

from us. Hoping that they understand his message, his life, and his invitation to faith, Jesus gives his disciples the chance to declare their faith. Within the question itself, he offers a clue to the answer by invoking God's name: "I Am." He hints that he is the face of God. Indeed, if we have ears to hear, he gives us the answer.

Peter blurts out an answer—but he has no idea what he is saying. "You are the Messiah," Peter responds. He thinks Jesus is a revolutionary liberator sent by God to lead Israel in military warfare against the Romans, reclaiming Jerusalem by violent revolt. He wants Jesus to take charge of the struggle, to become their political-military leader, and to assert Israel's pre-ordained, political domination. Peter's type of "messiah" reflects the empire—a messiah that uses the same imperial force to claim his imperial reign. Peter cannot imagine the "I Am" lurking in the question standing before him.

Jesus will have none of it, however. "Tell no one about me," he warns Peter and the gang. He knows they do not understand who he is, what he is about, or what lies ahead for them, and he does not want them spreading the wrong message, that he is an imperial messiah who will soon take charge and set things straight. So he tells them plainly: He is going to suffer, to be rejected, persecuted, arrested, tried, tortured, and executed—and three days later, he will rise again.

Peter is shocked and the conversation spirals out of control. No one should undergo such brutality, certainly not the Messiah of God. "Jesus does not understand what it means to be messiah," Peter thinks. "He does not realize the political-military opportunity for victory." Peter will never allow such a disaster, so he rebukes Jesus: "Heaven forbid!"

We are told that Jesus turns and looks at the disciples. This detail implies that Jesus has his back to Peter when Peter rebukes him. Now Jesus turns and faces Peter and the disciples. He has heard this temptation to imperial domination before, when he was tempted in the desert by Satan. So he rebukes Peter: "Get behind me, Satan. You are thinking not as God does, but as human beings do."

So much for pious conversation, political reflection, and Peter's proud declarations!

Mark uses the same word *rebuke* when Jesus silences the demons (see 1:25 and 3:12) and the wind (see 4:39). He deliberately has Jesus speak of himself not as "the Messiah," but as Daniel's "Son of Humanity," or "Human One." Jesus realistically faces the confrontation that awaits him at the end of the road in Jerusalem. He sees that his prophetic truth-telling can only lead to rejection by the elders, chief priests, and scribes. More than that, he knows the Book of Daniel and the prophet Isaiah. He sees himself as God's "Servant of Justice" (see Isaiah 42), a Suffering Servant (see Isaiah 53).

"Get behind me, Satan. You are thinking not as God does, but as human beings do." Jesus thinks as God does; Peter and the disciples do not. We do not. Jesus walks the narrow path of nonviolence to suffering, torture, death, and beyond—to new life. The disciples do not; we do not. We do not even understand it. Like Peter and the gang, we think like other human beings. We avoid suffering, run from the cross, and despise risky nonviolence and the consequences of persecution, suffering, arrest, imprisonment, and death. Jesus accepts the cross because he thinks like God does.

Jesus sees himself not just as the beloved of God, but as one who is rejected, who suffers, who is tortured and killed, and who rises from death. He risks suffering, undergoes death, rises from death, and overcomes death. He focuses on the essentials: life, death, life after death.

After this rebuke and counter-rebuke, Jesus summons the crowd and the disciples and explains, in no uncertain terms, what discipleship requires and why discipleship fulfills human life:

> "Whoever wishes to come after me must deny himself [or herself], take up [the] cross, and follow me. For whoever wishes to save his [or her] life will lose it, but whoever loses his [or her] life for my sake and that of the gospel will save it. What profit is there for one to gain the whole world and forfeit his [or her] life? What could one give in exchange for his [or her] life?" (Mark 8:34–37)

Jesus is a nonviolent Messiah and, in a world of imperial violence, such luminous nonviolence gets quickly quashed. But he insists that anyone—whether one of the disciples or a bystander in the crowd—who wishes to follow him must risk the same luminous nonviolence, into suffering and martyrdom.

The Gospel asks us "Who is Jesus?" Jesus is the one who carries the cross of nonviolent resistance and love. Followers of Jesus, therefore, also carry the cross of nonviolent resistance and love. They risk suffering and death, undergo suffering and death, rise above suffering and death, and overcome suffering and death. Like their Savior, followers of Jesus do not seek power or domination. They do not "lord it over others or make their authority felt" (cf. Mark 10:42). Rather, they follow a nonviolent Messiah, the Incarnation of Suffering Love, who resists the world's forces of death by undergoing death. In pursuit of the truth of God's nonviolent reign, they become incarnations of suffering love, resist the world's forces of death, and undergo suffering, like the Messiah, rather than inflict it on others.

No wonder Peter balks! Jesus identifies himself as a martyr of nonviolence, the Messiah of nonviolence. Peter recoils at the realization that the one who has captured his imagination, the one he follows, shall soon be martyred. What's more, this future martyr requires that his followers also risk martyrdom for nonviolent resistance to injustice. Markan scholar Ched Myers sums up the exchange:

> Jesus has revealed that his messiaship means political confrontation with, not rehabilitation of, the imperial state. Those who wish to "come after him" will have to identify themselves with his subversive program. The stated risk is that the disciple will face the test of loyalty under interrogation by state authorities. If "self" is denied, the cross will be taken up, a metaphor for capital punishment on grounds of insurgency. Through these definitive choices, the disciples will follow Jesus.[1]

In explaining who he is and what he will undergo, Jesus asks more ultimate questions: "What profit is there for one to gain the whole world and forfeit his [or her] life? What could one give in exchange for his [or her] life?" (Mark 8:36–37) Jesus sees an underlying imperial ambition in Peter's assertion. If we want to follow Jesus, we will have to renounce our ambitions and even our lives. Then we will find life. Then we will be disciples. Then we will know who Jesus is.

His questions haunt us. The culture insists that nothing could be greater than "making it" in the world. If we become president, senator, corporate C.E.O., rich, or famous, then we have found life. But the one who thinks as God thinks knows that those who gain the world have forfeited their lives. In contrast, those who appear as utter failures in the eyes of the culture actually save their lives. Those who suffer and die powerless on the margins, in shelters, prisons, hospitals, refugee camps, death rows, or other Golgathas, like Jesus on the cross, will live on in God's anti-imperial reign. If we die as Jesus dies, if we remain faithful to God and God's way of service and love, we shall rise and gain our lives.

Jesus' question, *"Who do you say that I am?"* challenges us to take up our cross and walk the narrow path of nonviolence. It invites us to the truth—that life is not found in worldly success but in suffering love on behalf of God's reign. It pushes us to know Christ and ourselves in the struggle for justice and peace. It summons us to live as Christ lived, to die as Christ died, to rise as Christ rose and, in the process, to discover the mystery of our own identity as God's children. It asks us who we are, who we see ourselves to be, and who we are willing to become. In the new, divine light of his shining example, we have the strength to see ourselves as his nonviolent followers, daughters and sons of God, peacemakers. Then we will have the courage to say, "You, Jesus, are the living God of peace, the God who suffers and dies and rises, the God of nonviolence."

chapter sixteen

THE GOOD SAMARITAN

"Who is my neighbor?" Jesus replied, "A man fell victim to robbers as he went down from Jerusalem to Jericho. They stripped and beat him and went off leaving him half-dead. A priest happened to be going down that road, but when he saw him, he passed by on the opposite side. Likewise a Levite came to the place, and when he saw him, he passed by on the opposite side. But a Samaritan traveler who came upon him was moved with compassion at the sight. He approached the victim, poured oil and wine over his wounds and bandaged them. Then he lifted him up on his own animal, took him to an inn and cared for him. The next day he took out two silver coins and gave them to the innkeeper with the instruction, 'Take care of him. If you spend more than what I have given you, I shall repay you on my way back.' Which of these three, in your opinion, was neighbor to the robbers' victim?" He answered, "The one who treated him with mercy." Jesus said to him, "Go and do likewise." (Luke 10:29–37)

In October 1992, on the 500th anniversary of Columbus' arrival and the subsequent genocide of the native peoples, I traveled around Haiti for two weeks. One year earlier, a CIA-backed military coup had left over four thousand people dead and some fifty thousand Haitians in exile, including the popular president, Jean-Bertrande Aristide.

That autumn our delegation journeyed through Port-au-Prince, to Cap Haitien in the north, and into several villages, where we witnessed the grinding poverty and listened to dozens of underground priests, sisters, and Christians in hiding speak of their work for justice. At the conclusion of our journey, we testified before the Organization of American States' observers team about the death threats, repressive violence, and human rights violations.

The night before our group flew from Miami to Port-au-Prince, we gathered in a church basement and opened our Bibles to the story of the Good Samaritan. We read the parable out loud, sat in silent prayer, and then spoke about our pending journey within the context of the parable. The suffering, persecuted poor of Haiti are our neighbors, and they lie in a ditch bleeding. Can we North Americans—the enemy of the Haitian poor—be Good Samaritans and act with love, compassion, and mercy toward our sisters and brothers in Haiti? We prayed that God would fashion us into truly compassionate neighbors to the suffering people of Haiti.

With a population of over six million people, the poorest country in the hemisphere, Haiti is the home of hunger and disease. Over 85% of the people of Haiti live in poverty. Four-tenths of one percent of the population own 43% of the wealth, with annual incomes over one million dollars, while 17% of the population has annual incomes under $300. Seventy-five percent of the people live in the countryside and depend on agriculture for their livelihood. Only 2% of the rural population has access to safe water, and most families do not have electricity or running water. More than half the population has no sanitary facilities, and at least one-third of all the children suffer from malnutrition. A Haitian child dies every five minutes.

One of our most memorable and shocking experiences was a visit to Cite Soleil, Haiti's poorest slum on the edge of Port-au-Prince, where at least half a million people suffer destitution. Muddy, stinking ditches filled with excrement separate the endless shacks of wood, cardboard, and tin. Naked children play with pigs in the ditches, and trash piles up everywhere. There is no running water, no sewage, no bathrooms, and no electricity.

Within minutes after our arrival, thousands of ragged, smiling people crowded around us to touch and greet us—for few North Americans visit their slum. Although their lives were filled with misery, their eyes radiated gentleness and life. In the midst of their agony, they possess deep faith, determined hope, and selfless love. Certainly the God of the poor lives and dies among the suffering people of Cite Soleil. Like the City of Joy outside Calcutta, this hovel has become a place where Jesus suffers, dies, and rises again. These oppressed people know that the Spirit of Christ is in their midst, and so they struggle to live.

"Who is my neighbor?" the legal scholar asks Jesus. His response, the parable of the Good Samaritan, paints a portrait of gruesome indifference and radiant compassion. Someone has been beaten and left to die in a ditch by the side of the road. The religious elite, symbolized by a priest and a Levite, see the suffering victim and turn away "from the sight." They respond to the face of suffering by walking to the opposite side of the road so that they do not have to make eye contact with the suffering person.

Then along comes a Samaritan, the hated enemy of the Judeans in Jesus' day. Unlike the priest and the Levite, the Samaritan is "moved with compassion at the sight"; he does not turn away or walk to the opposite side of the road. Rather, he looks into the eyes of the suffering person and, in that human exchange, he recognizes the humanity and the dignity of the suffering victim in the ditch. Perhaps the Samaritan can identify with the suffering person because he, too, has been the victim of violence. At some point, he, too, probably felt ostracized if not scorned and hated by the neighboring Judeans, including priests and Levites. In any case, his heart responds to the sight of suffering—and he takes action.

The Good Samaritan interrupts his journey to care for the one who is suffering. While the priest and the Levite do not have time for the poor, the Good Samaritan makes time. He approaches the victim, pours oil and wine over his wounds, bandages them, lifts him on to his animal, takes him to an inn, cares for him, watches over him through the night, pays for his room and board, and promises to look in on him upon his return. His concern is personal, whole-hearted, and sacrificial.

"Which of these three, in your opinion, was neighbor to the robbers' victim?" Jesus asks the legal scholar.

"The one who treated him with compassion," he answers.

"Go and do likewise," Jesus concludes.

Jesus would have us reach out, one on one, to those who fall victim to violence. He wants all of us to live the loving kindness that we reserve for Saint Francis and Mother Teresa. He calls those of us who live in First World countries to show social compassion to suffering Third and Fourth World peoples, such as the suffering poor of Haiti. He wants us to turn our attention and resources to the suffering people of Cite Soleil and all the Cite Soleils of the world, to lift them out of the ditch and relieve them of their pain. He insists that we interrupt our busy day-to-day lives, make contact with the faces of poverty, and take action. He wants us to be true neighbors to one another—to love one another.

Jesus complicates his story by portraying the hated enemy as the one who acts with compassion, suggesting that those who practice the compassion of Jesus are often those we least expect—our hated enemies! If we imagine ourselves as the person in the ditch, the implications deepen as we picture our enemy as the one who saves us! On the other hand, the religious elite—whom the culture upholds as the most godly—do not fair well in Jesus' estimation.

One cannot help but notice that Luke's parable foreshadows Jesus' own torture and crucifixion. Jesus becomes the suffering person left to die in a roadside ditch. Who will reach out with compassion to him? Who will stop the authorities and soldiers from legally beating and killing him? No one. He dies on the cross. And he continues to suffer and die in ditches, roadsides, and hovels around the world—from Haiti to the South Bronx, from Calcutta to death row, from Baghdad to South Central L.A. Will we walk around him, like the priest and the Levite, and permit the suffering and killing to continue—or will we look at him in those who suffer, allow our hearts to be moved with compassion, lift him from the ditch, tend to the wounds, pay for room and board, and commence the healing process?

The parable ends with a new commandment: "Go and do likewise."

chapter seventeen

DIVES AND LAZARUS

"There was a rich man who dressed in purple garments and fine linen and dined sumptuously each day. And lying at his door was a poor man named Lazarus, covered with sores, who would gladly have eaten his fill of the scraps that fell from the rich man's table. Dogs even used to come and lick his sores. When the poor man died, he was carried away by angels to the bosom of Abraham. The rich man also died and was buried, and from the netherworld, where he was in torment, he raised his eyes and saw Abraham far off and Lazarus at his side. And he cried out, 'Father Abraham, have pity on me. Send Lazarus to dip the tip of his finger in water and cool my tongue, for I am suffering torment in these flames.' Abraham replied, 'My child, remember that you received what was good during your lifetime while Lazarus likewise received what was bad; but now he is comforted here, whereas you are tormented. Moreover, between us and you a great chasm is established to prevent anyone from crossing who might wish to go from our side to yours or from your side to ours.' He said, 'Then I beg you, father, send him to my father's house, for I have five brothers, so that he may warn them, lest they too come to this place of torment.' But Abraham replied, 'They have Moses and the proph-ets. Let them listen to them.' He said, 'Oh no, father Abraham, but if someone from the dead goes to them, they will repent.' Then Abraham said, 'If they will not listen to Moses and the prophets, neither will they be persuaded if someone should rise from the dead.'" (Luke 16:19–31)

While living in New York City and teaching theology at Fordham University, I often celebrated an evening Eucharist with the New York Catholic Worker community. One winter evening we gathered in the small chapel at Maryhouse, the women's house of hospitality where Dorothy Day lived and died. There in that holy space, during the 1970s, Day joined other Catholic Workers to pray the Liturgy of the Hours every morning and evening. After her death in November 1980, her body was placed in a handmade pine coffin on a long, dark, wooden table that served as an altar in the center of the room.

That winter night, as I entered the chapel and saw the wooden chairs along the wall and the wooden altar in the center of the room, I thought of Dorothy Day and her lifelong, selfless service to the marginalized poor. I greeted old friends who, like Day, have lived lives of service and hospitality. As the liturgy began, we introduced ourselves to one another, then listened to the Scriptures, broke bread, and passed the cup. It was an evening of grace and peace, and I was blessed to be in that company, among the homeless and those who live in community with them as servants and workers. I stood on holy ground, among modern-day good Samaritans, in a city of priests and Levites.

The Gospel that evening was both a challenge and a comfort: Luke's parable of Dives and Lazarus. Lazarus spent his life in abject poverty at the doorstep of Dives (Latin for "rich man") and found comfort in heaven resting in Abraham. Dives, however, spent his life in comfort and security on earth, and found suffering in the next world. They both lived. They both died. The only one who could affect the status of both of them was the rich man, who could have fed and comforted the poor man. Instead, he chose not to offer comfort, and so continued the suffering of the poor man and insured his own eventual suffering.

After the reading, we sat in silence. What can one say about such a parable? It stands as one of the harshest readings in the Scriptures. No wonder so few of us cite it, discuss it, or refer to it. Perhaps it hits so hard because we First World North Americans identify not with the suffering Lazarus but—rightly—with the comfortable, well-dressed, well-fed Dives. Does that mean that because we do not house the homeless, feed the hungry, and comfort the miserable, we are headed for the fires of torment, like Dives? One does not like to contemplate such a scalding message yet, the implications of this shocking tale are frightening: Unless we change our lives, relinquish our wealth, serve those in need, end suffering, and bring comfort and joy to those in pain, we will end up in fiery torment. That night at the Catholic Worker, we bowed our heads in silence. Although the story stopped our hearts, we felt pushed to hear it, to take its life-or-death urgency to heart, and to let it change our lives.

In this parable, Luke offers the flip side of the parable of the Good Samaritan, where Jesus tells us how to respond humanly to the suffering of another—by showing compassion, stopping our journey, helping those in need, going out of our way to relieve the suffering of someone we do not even know, spending our own resources to insure the other's healing. In the parable of Dives and Lazarus, Jesus pointedly describes what happens to us when we do not reach out to those in need—when we fail to be the Good Samaritan. The tables get reversed. We sow the seeds of our own affliction, and the outcome is in our own hands.

Like Dickens's *A Christmas Carol,* the parable of Dives and Lazarus makes a specific point: What we do or do not do to relieve the sufferings of the poor around us has consequences for God's reign here and now and for eternal life. This urgent message, then, can be taken as a word of warning and a word of hope.

As a word of warning, the Gospel pleads with us to go out into the streets, pick up the suffering poor, feed them, clothe them, shelter them, heal them, welcome them into our lives, share our material wealth with them, and help end suffering—one person at a time. By ignoring the suffering of the poor around us, we insure the "early and unjust death of the poor" here and now in this life, as theologian Jon Sobrino puts it, and our own suffering in the next life.

As a word of hope, this parable offers good news to the poor. God sees their suffering; God does not will it, and God does not bless it. God does not want anyone to suffer in poverty, hunger, misery, or homelessness. God is actively liberating the suffering poor from oppression and injustice, and seeks people to assist the work of compassion, liberation, and justice. But God sees not only the suffering and oppression of the poor; God also sees the callous indifference of the comfortable. God knows that we, the comfortable, can never be our full human selves until we share our hearts and resources with those in need, risking our worldly comforts and security. We deepen our spiritual lives by comforting the afflicted, sharing our comforts with one another, and preventing the affliction of others. God wants us to wake up, break through our apathy, shake off our lethargy, let go of our comforts, and spend our days bringing relief and justice to the suffering poor. Indeed, God wants us to risk our lives in the nonviolent struggle for justice and peace for the whole human race. Our conversion will relieve the poor from physical misery and ourselves from spiritual anomie.

Dorothy Day embraced this gospel challenge more than most Christians. She and Peter Maurin opened houses of hospitality for thousands of Lazaruses who languished on the streets of First World North America. Day then made the connection between the suffering poor she served and the culture that actively oppressed them into poverty and misery. The culture does not just ignore the plight of the poor, she declaimed. It actively cuts welfare assistance, affordable housing, food stamps, and decent healthcare and employment opportunities. It bulldozes shantytowns and arrests the homeless so that the consciences of the rich will not be bothered as they go shopping. It spends trillions of dollars on weapons of war and deliberately inflicts suffering upon the poor, at home and abroad. Indeed, the culture oppresses millions of people around the world into poverty through its military expenditures, and plans their murder in war. Over two hundred million human beings have died from warfare in this century alone. The world turns people into suffering Lazaruses and kills them. Dorothy Day saw this inhumanity and declared that we must not only relieve the suffering of the poor on our doorsteps, but we must resist the system that kills the poor.

"The Christian ideal has not been tried and found wanting," Chesterton wrote long ago. "It has been found difficult and left untried." Our Gospel heralds a hard but beautiful message. It demands dedication to the poor and a committed struggle for justice. Luke suggests that if we heed the message of Moses and the prophets—indeed, if we accept the resurrection of Christ—then we will live serving others as the Good Samaritan did, as Jesus did. Not only will we relieve the suffering of the poor and comfort the afflicted, we will give our lives for the struggle for justice and peace.

If we do not heed the message of Moses and the prophets, if we do not repent of our complicity with injustice, Luke warns, we will not respond to the needs of the poor even if someone should rise from the dead urging us to pursue God's reign. One presumes that if someone rose from the dead, our lives would be changed; everything would be different. All our assumptions would be thrown out the window, and we would no longer fear death. Rather, we would dedicate our lives to the selfless service of all and promote life for all people, including the poor and our enemies. We would know that life continues beyond death—in other words, that life begins now and our eternal life is bound up in the compassionate service of those in need.

Luke concludes his good news by announcing that, in fact, Jesus, who was crucified by the Roman authorities, has risen from the dead. His friends saw him, ate with him, and experienced joy in his presence. To accept Luke's message of Jesus' resurrection means to heed the warning of Dives: to feed the hungry at our doorstep and stop the culture from killing the poor.

If we let the risen Jesus touch us with his compassion, we will be moved with compassion for the needy. We will become people of resurrection who oppose the forces of death that oppress people and leave them dying to be licked by passing dogs. The Resurrection transforms us to give our lives in peace for others, beginning with the poor, the victims of war.

As we put the parable into action and reach out to serve and then defend the Lazaruses of this world, the culture will crack down on us and we will ultimately share the fate of Lazarus, the prophets, and the crucified Jesus. We, too, will suffer and die, but we know that life does not end there. We will also share the Resurrection.

chapter eighteen

TRANSFIGURATION

*[Jesus] took Peter, John, and James and went up the mountain to pray.
While he was praying his face changed in appearance and his clothing
became dazzling white. And behold, two men were conversing with him,
Moses and Elijah, who appeared in glory and spoke of his exodus that he
was going to accomplish in Jerusalem. Peter and his companions had
been overcome by sleep, but becoming fully awake, they saw his glory and
the two men standing with him. As they were about to part from him,
Peter said to Jesus, "Master, it is good that we are here; let us make three
tents, one for you, one for Moses, and one for Elijah." But he did not
know what he was saying. While he was still speaking, a cloud came and
cast a shadow over them, and they became frightened when they entered
the cloud. Then from the cloud came a voice that said, "This is my chosen
Son; listen to him." After the voice had spoken, Jesus was found alone.
They fell silent and did not at that time tell anyone what they had seen.
(Luke 9:28–36)*

August 6, the anniversary of the U.S. atomic bombing of Hiroshima,
marks the Feast of the Transfiguration. When read in the context of
the nuclear blast over Hiroshima, the Transfiguration of Jesus takes on a
whole new meaning. The Gospel not only shows us the flip side of our
nuclear violence in the nonviolence of Jesus, but it offers us a way out of
our insanity.

Jesus is heading toward Jerusalem. In Luke's account, he has just taught
his friends that they must love their enemies and take up the cross of nonviolent resistance to evil. He knows his days are numbered—that the authorities
are planning to kill him because he speaks out against injustice—and he un-
dertakes one last side trip before the final leg of his journey. With three
friends, he climbs the mountain for a few days of prayer and solitude.

Luke opens the story of the Transfiguration with Jesus praying alone on the mountaintop. We could contemplate this scene of Jesus praying in solitude for the rest of our lives—but the story continues. In this contemplative moment, Jesus' clothes become "dazzlingly" white, a biblical sign of martyrdom. Moses and Elijah appear, representing the law and the prophets and summing up the whole spiritual tradition. Together, they encourage Jesus to walk the path of nonviolent resistance from the mountaintop to the cross.

At this dramatic highpoint in the spiritual life of Jesus, we might ask, "Where are the disciples, his friends Peter, John, and James? How are they supporting Christ? What can we learn from them about how to support Christ on his journey of transfiguring nonviolence?" Luke tells us that at this profound revelation of Jesus' inner mystical life, the disciples rest, off to the side, sound asleep. Here we have the ultimate image of the male-dominated Church—off to the side, sleeping through the Transfiguration. We churchmen have been sleeping for two thousand years.

When they awake, the disciples realize the meaning of Jesus' prayer and instantly start objecting to Jesus' way of nonviolent resistance—and the objections are so telling. Instead of comforting Jesus and encouraging him on his peacemaking journey, like Moses and Elijah do, Peter blurts out: "Master, it is good for *us* to be here." The disciples are so egotistic; they speak only about themselves. They are never really concerned for Jesus. If they were, Peter would affirm Jesus as Moses and Elijah do. He would tell Jesus how good it is for *Jesus* to be there at this moment of consolation and confirmation by the holy ones—before he embarks to his execution.

Instead, Peter tries to get control of the situation. "Forget the cross and suffering and death," Peter says in effect, "Let's build some houses here, maybe a retreat center, and stay here forever, far away from Jerusalem and the Temple, from the world and its injustice."

There is a part of Peter lurking in all of us, more concerned for ourselves, our egos, and our own fate than for Jesus as he goes to the cross. Like Peter, we all have a comfortable mountaintop place where we think we have God under control, where we want to stay forever, far away from our own Jerusalems. Like Peter, we try to control Jesus.

The reaction of Peter and the other disciples to Jesus' contemplative nonviolence points to the spiritual crisis that confronts us today. Instead of accompanying Jesus (and thus one another) on his way of nonviolent suffering love—the way of the cross—we try to stop him, to remain on the comfortable mountaintop far removed from Jerusalem. Even with the beatific vision of Moses and Elijah standing before him, Peter tries to dissuade Jesus from the cross by insisting that Jesus stay put and listen to him. He thinks, like we all do, that he knows better than Jesus. "If only Jesus would listen to us," we tell each other. Instead of accompanying Jesus back down the mountain into the messy confrontation with the authorities and its bloody outcome, we resist Jesus, we disobey Jesus and, eventually, like the disciples, we run away from Jesus.

Just at this moment, as Peter tries to prevent Jesus from going to Jerusalem, a cloud comes and overshadows them. The voice of God speaks from the cloud, gently telling the terrified disciples, "This is my beloved. Listen to him." God does not condemn Peter. Rather, God tells the disciples to *listen* to Jesus. The Transfiguration invites us to be people of contemplative prayer, people who listen attentively to Jesus and, thus, people who can accompany Jesus on his journey from the mountaintop to the cross.

Here we have one of the clearest and most neglected commands of the Scriptures. "Jesus is my beloved. Listen to him." Here lies the great lesson of the Gospel: God's message to us after Hiroshima and Nagasaki, God's way out of our nuclear madness, God's blueprint for the next millennium of discipleship in gospel nonviolence. Today, the God of peace is saying to us, "The nonviolent Jesus is my beloved; listen to him. Become people of contemplative prayer. Be people who listen attentively to Jesus."

When we listen to Jesus, we hear a message with definite political and social ramifications: "Love one another. Love your enemies. Forgive one another. Be compassionate. Be merciful. Seek God's reign and God's justice. Put away the sword. Rise and do not be afraid." When we listen to Jesus, when we meditate on his word and attend to his voice, we are transfigured.

If we obey this command, if we take time for daily prayer and sit quietly listening to Jesus, our hearts will be disarmed of our inner violence. We will put down our swords and renounce our violence. We will beat our swords into plowshares, love our enemies, and pledge never to study war again. We will dismantle every nuclear and conventional weapon of destruction and spend our resources alleviating human suffering. We will be transfigured into people of contemplative nonviolence. We will become, like Jesus, people who listen to God. When we listen to Jesus' voice, we will finally discover new strength to go down the mountain into the world with the good news of love. We, too, will be willing to undergo the paschal mystery for the sake of justice, disarmament, and peace. We, too, will sacrifice ourselves for the sake of suffering humanity.

Our Gospel sums up for us the contrast between Jesus and the God of nonviolence, and ourselves and our desire to dominate others, which is at the root of all violence, especially our nuclear crimes. The Transfiguration portrays the inner power of Jesus' transforming nonviolence—pure love, perfect peace, unconditional mercy, and steadfast resistance to the forces of violence. In the Transfiguration, Jesus radiates perfect nonviolence, and we glimpse the glorious face of the God of peace. We begin to understand who Jesus is and what it means to follow him. Through his inner prayer, Jesus undergoes a spiritual explosion of peace and love that leads him to resist the structures of injustice—even to the point of death—and reveals the God of nonviolence.

The U.S. atomic bombings of Hiroshima and Nagasaki, on the other hand, reveal the exact opposite of God's transfiguring nonviolence. They epitomize our disfiguring violence. Dorothy Day called the bombing of Hiroshima an "anti-transfiguration." She read this Gospel from the perspective of the bomb, with its bright flash of white light, its mushroom cloud, and its nuclear fireball incinerating our sisters and brothers. In Jesus, she saw the possibility of humanity's transfiguration through the way of prayerful nonviolence. With Hiroshima, she saw our preference for disfiguring violence.

Dorothy Day understood the importance of prayerful listening. She spent her days quietly listening to the words of Jesus, and this prayerful attention to Jesus transfigured her life. She lived her years serving Christ in the poor and speaking out against the wars and weapons that threaten to kill us all. Day's contemplative nonviolence made her an instrument of Christ's peace. Without her prayerful listening, the Catholic Worker would not have been started—and would not continue to flourish today.

Where is Jesus speaking to us today? If we listen closely, we can hear Jesus:

❖ in the silence of the ashes of Hiroshima and Nagasaki;

❖ in the voices of the Hibakusha, the atomic bomb survivors who call for total nuclear disarmament and the abolition of war;

❖ in the laughter, longings, and cries of the world's children, who look to us for peace;

❖ in the pleas of our enemies, who long to be loved by us;

❖ in the poor and the marginalized, who suffer the fallout of our six-hundred-billion-dollar budget for war;

❖ in the cry of liberation from the imprisoned, the tortured, the homeless, the hungry, the ill and the dying;

❖ in the voices from death row, who call for the abolition of the death penalty;

❖ in the dead of Rwanda, Bosnia, Palestine, Iraq, Sudan, Central America, South Africa, Northern Ireland, and our own city streets, who cry out, "Stop the killing, stop the bombings, stop the violence";

❖ in all those who differ from us, who call us beyond the blindness of racism to the vision of a reconciled humanity, the beloved community;

❖ in the faithful women of the world who, unlike the somnolent male disciples, remain wide awake, announcing a paradigmatic shift, the fall of patriarchy, and the birth of a just Church;

❖ in the solitude of creation, from the mountaintops to the oceans; in the gentle rain and silent breeze that call us to praise the God of peace, the God of Life;

❖ in our own hearts, in our breath, in our prayer, telling us how much God loves us all, telling us that we, too, are God's beloved sons and daughters, inviting us all to be transfigured in love so that we can go forward down the mountain to the cross in a spirit of love.

Peace becomes possible only if we listen to the voice of Jesus. As we spend our lives listening every day for the voice of God, we find ourselves transformed and, over time, we become contemplatives. As we hear the God of peace speak to us, we are filled with peace. We are disarmed and, without our knowing it, we are transformed into God's instruments for the disarmament of the world.

Today we name our government's crucifixion of Hiroshima and Nagasaki not just sinful, unjust, and immoral, but demonic—an evil act by a people (ourselves) possessed by the spirits of violence. We apologize to the people of Hiroshima and Nagasaki for vaporizing them and unleashing the nuclear age and, in a spirit of repentance, we pledge ourselves anew to the pursuit of nuclear disarmament, the abolition of war, and a world without weapons or hunger. We promise, from now on, to listen to the gentle voice of the God of nonviolence.

There is hope after all. The Transfiguration offers us a way out.

All we have to do is listen.

chapter nineteen

THE RICH YOUNG MAN

As [Jesus] was setting out on a journey, a man ran up, knelt down before him, and asked him, "Good teacher, what must I do to inherit eternal life?" Jesus answered him, "Why do you call me good? No one is good but God alone. You know the commandments: 'You shall not kill; you shall not commit adultery; you shall not steal; you shall not bear false witness; you shall not defraud; honor your father and your mother.'" He replied and said to him, "Teacher, all of these I have observed from my youth." Jesus, looking at him, loved him and said to him, "You are lacking in one thing. Go, sell what you have, and give to (the) poor and you will have treasure in heaven; then come, follow me." At that statement his face fell, and he went away sad, for he had many possessions. (Mark 10:17–22)

Every applicant to the Society of Jesus is asked to write a ten-page autobiographical essay. Before I began my reflection, in 1981, I read through the Gospels trying to find a passage that spoke to my life journey and my decision to follow Jesus as a Jesuit priest. I came upon the story of the rich young man (or, according to Mark's version, the rich man). As I pondered this story, I realized that I wanted to do what the rich man was unable to do: I wanted to sell what I had, give to the poor, and follow Jesus. That became the theme of my essay—and my life journey.

Now, years later, I ponder the economic security that my religious community provides. Most institutional religious orders like the Jesuits possess large bank accounts and enormous land holdings. Our wealth keeps us from entering God's reign. My friends and I try to live simply, to walk among the poor, to break through the world's false security, and to pay the price of costly discipleship. I am still trying to do what the rich young man could not do—to follow Jesus completely. And I have a long way to go.

The story of the rich man applies directly to us First World Christians. We live comfortably, and are proud, arrogant, and self-righteous. Like the rich man, some of us are obsessed with getting into heaven. We ask one another what is required to inherit eternal life. Like the rich man, we want God to tell us what we have to do to inherit eternal life, as if it is something we achieve, something we earn, something we deserve.

The rich man interrupts Jesus' journey. To get Jesus' attention and to justify himself, he begins by flattering Jesus. But he asks the wrong question or, at least, he puts it badly. Jesus responds openly, urging obedience to God's commandments: "Do not kill. Do not commit adultery. Do not steal. Do not commit false witness. Honor your father and your mother."

Keeping these commandments, especially the first, is indeed a noble accomplishment. Jesus, however, adds a new commandment to the list, perhaps to test the man: "Do not defraud." Although the rich man insists that he has kept all these commandments, he misses Jesus' new commandment that forbids greed, oppression of the poor, and complicity with economic injustice. The rich man does not realize that his wealth violates this commandment.

But Jesus does not get angry with the man. For the first time in the Scriptures, we are told that Jesus looks on someone "with love." Despite the man's blindness, self-righteousness, and indifference to the poor, Jesus feels compassion for him. In Luke's account, Jesus practices what he has just preached: He loves his enemies. In this compassionate love, he issues one of the great invitations of Scripture: "You are lacking in one thing. Go, sell what you have, and give to (the) poor and you will have treasure in heaven; then come, follow me" (Mark 10:21). The man walks away crestfallen for, we are finally told, he has many possessions.

Several verses later, Mark relates the encounter between the blind beggar, Bartimaeus, and Jesus. Hearing that Jesus is passing by, Bartimaeus calls out to him—and Jesus stops. He tells those around him to call to Bartimaeus and, we are told, the blind man immediately throws aside his cloak and goes to Jesus. Because Bartimaeus is a helpless beggar, his cloak holds the coins he receives as a result of his begging. Yet, at the invitation of Jesus, he throws away the cloak and, with it, all his money. He has no possessions! In response to such disregard for money and such a passionate desire for God's mercy, Jesus asks, "What do you want me to do for you?"

Instead of asking for eternal life, the blind man asks for vision. In response, Jesus says, "Go your way; your faith has saved you" (Mark 10:51–52). As he receives his sight, Bartimaeus follows Jesus on the way to the cross.

These two contrasting stories reveal the attitude of the wealthy and the poor toward the gospel of Jesus. By and large, the poor have nothing to lose and everything to gain as they seek Christ. They grasp his invitation, focus wholeheartedly on Christ, and eagerly follow him on the way. However, we First World Christians, like the rich man, find it hard to let go of our possessions. We have been inculturated into America's demonic spirit of greed—and have been consumed by our consumerism. Our possessions control not only our lives but our souls, preventing us, even unknowingly, from following Jesus. We end up asking God the wrong questions, assuming we can control God, believing that eternal life belongs to us as an inheritance. All the while we fail to recognize our blindness and never ask for vision. In the end, we never see Jesus in the poor or follow him on the way of the cross.

There are exceptions, of course. One thinks of Saint Francis, the hope and pride of Assisi, who abandoned his father's business and possessions for a life of poverty and discipleship. One reflects on Martin Luther King, Jr., the son of an upper middle-class preacher, who renounced his privileged life and the possibility of a comfortable academic career to follow Jesus in the struggle for civil rights, economic justice, and peace. One ponders the journey of spiritual writer Henri Nouwen, who gave up tenured positions at Yale and Harvard to live and work in South America and finally to join the L'Arche-Daybreak community, where he spent ten years serving the disabled before his untimely death.

One recalls Jean Donovan, the twenty-seven-year-old Maryknoll lay missioner, assassinated with Sisters Ita Ford, Maura Clarke, and Dorothy Kazel in El Salvador in 1980. Jean grew up in an affluent, Republican, Connecticut household, but quit her accounting job, gave up her career goals, turned her attention to the Third World poor, and followed Jesus into war-torn Central America. Shortly before her brutal death, after the Peace Corps had left because of the increasing violence, Jean wrote to a friend:

Several times I have decided to leave El Salvador. I almost could except for the children, the poor, bruised victims of this insanity. Who would care for them? Whose heart could be so staunch as to favor the reasonable thing in a sea of their tears and loneliness? Not mine, dear friend, not mine.[1]

Dorothy Day lived a shining example of renouncing all for the one thing lacking: She gave everything she had to the poor, founded the Catholic Worker, spoke out for peace and disarmament, and spent her life following Jesus. As she approached her death, she was grateful for having kept Christ on her mind nearly every day of her life. As Daniel Berrigan once commented, Dorothy Day not only made the connection between the sufferings of the poor and the world's militarism, she lived the connections. In her Catholic Worker life, she practiced voluntary poverty, resisted war, and suffered persecution for her unpopular stand. Her response to the invitation of Jesus was wholehearted, complete, and steadfast. She suffered persecution, arrest, and jail for her faithful discipleship. She lived and died among the poor and, like Francis, her witness demonstrates the life of radical discipleship to Christ.

As we grapple with the invitation of Jesus and the example of those who have given up all for Christ, we notice Jesus' own interior attitude toward us, rich or poor. He puts himself completely at the disposal of the blind beggar, Bartimaeus: "What do you want me to do for you?" he asks. And he looks at the rich man with love. Surely he rejoices at the faith of the blind man, at his healing, and at his discipleship. Equally, he must feel the pangs of rejection as the rich man walks away from him.

Jesus takes a chance and invites discipleship. Yet, his offer is turned down. How many of us walk away from Jesus? How many of us continue to turn down his invitation and, instead, cling to our possessions? How does Jesus feel about the way we live our lives, our lukewarm discipleship, and our ongoing rejections of his ongoing invitations?

The Gospel's wisdom remains: "What good does it do to gain the whole world and lose one's soul?" Jesus asks (see Mark 8:36). In the long run, it does not profit us to horde possessions and reject Jesus' invitation.

So why not let it all go—give everything to the poor and follow Jesus? Why not keep on following him come what may? Like Bartimaeus, Francis,

Martin, Jean, and Dorothy, we, too, shall see. We, too, shall be blessed. We, too, can follow him on the way up the road to Jerusalem.

chapter twenty

THE ONCE-BLIND DISCIPLE

As [Jesus] passed by he saw a man blind from birth. His disciples asked him, "Rabbi, who sinned, this man or his parents, that he was born blind?" Jesus answered, "Neither he nor his parents sinned; it is so that the works of God might be made visible through him. We have to do the works of the one who sent me while it is day. Night is coming when no one can work. While I am in the world, I am the light of the world." When he had said this, he spat on the ground and made clay with the saliva, and smeared the clay on his eyes, and said to him, "Go wash in the Pool of Siloam" (which means Sent). So he went and washed, and came back able to see. . . . They brought the one who was once blind to the Pharisees. Now Jesus had made clay and opened his eyes on a sabbath. . . . The Jews did not believe that he had been blind and gained his sight until they summoned the parents of the one who had gained his sight. . . .

A second time they called the man who had been blind and said to him, "Give God the praise! We know that this man is a sinner." He replied, "If he is a sinner, I do not know. One thing I do know is that I was blind and now I see." So they said to him, "What did he do to you? How did he open your eyes?" He answered them, "I told you already and you did not listen. Why do you want to hear it again? Do you want to become his disciples, too?" They ridiculed him and said, "You are that man's disciple; we are disciples of Moses! We know that God spoke to Moses, but we do not know where this one is from." The man answered and said to them, "This is what is so amazing, that you do not know where he is from, yet he opened my eyes. We know that God does not listen to sinners, but if one is devout and does his will, he listens to him. It is unheard of that anyone ever opened the eyes of a person born blind. If this man were not from God, he would not be able to do anything." They answered and said to him, "You were born totally in sin, and are you trying to teach us?" Then they threw him out.

When Jesus heard that they had thrown him out, he found him and said, "Do you believe in the Son of Man?" He answered and said, "Who is he, sir, that I may believe in him?" Jesus said to him, "You have seen him and the one speaking with you is he." He said, "I do believe, Lord," and he worshiped him. Then Jesus said, "I came into this world for judgment, so that those who do not see might see, and those who do see might become blind." (John 9:1–39)

This story, which constitutes nearly all of John's ninth chapter, outlines the discipleship journey as perhaps no other story does. In the previous chapter of John's Gospel, Jesus saves the life of the woman caught in adultery by talking the hostile religious authorities out of stoning her to death. Then, in a long discourse with the Pharisees, he faces the charge of blasphemy and insists that he is telling the truth. "I am not possessed," he tells them. "I do not seek my own glory; there is one who seeks it and he is the one who judges . . . I say to you, whoever keeps my word will never see death" (John 8:49–51). When they ask if he has seen Abraham, he testifies, "Before Abraham came to be, I AM" (John 8:58). They immediately pick up stones to throw at him, but he manages to escape. He survives this assassination attempt by the theologians but, in effect, is kicked out of the Temple.

In this life-and-death context, Jesus notices the man born blind.

The opening line of our story in the original Greek makes a universal statement. Jesus walks by and sees not just one man but *humanity* born blind. Everyone is blind except Jesus, who sees clearly that none of us can see at all. It is a bold assertion. In response, his disciples pose as theologians and ask the age-old question, "Why do people suffer?" In pursuit of their ethical theories, they cite this poor blind man as Exhibit A. "In this case, who is at fault, this man or his parents, that he should be born blind?" Like the Pharisees, they muse about the sin of others, blind to their own sinfulness. They sound like the Pharisees and want to engage Jesus, as the Pharisees had done earlier that day, in lofty talk about imponderable questions. Notice they show no concern for the blind man or for Jesus, who has just missed being stoned to death by the theologians!

The question of suffering does not originate with Jesus. He sees our common blindness and the individual born blind "as an opportunity for God to be glorified." These appear at first glance as harsh words. Is Jesus a callous bystander who does not care about the suffering of others? Not at all. Although it sounds as if he spiritualizes other people's problems, he and only he takes action to heal the suffering of others. The disciples, on the other hand, with their lofty question, sound interested and concerned but, like the Pharisees, do nothing to heal the poor man's blindness. They show no compassion or concern for the poor blind beggar or for Jesus. They merely assert their own egos by philosophizing at the expense of the poor.

Jesus explains:

> "Neither he nor his parents sinned; it is so that the works of God might be made visible through him. We have to do the works of the one who sent me while it is day. Night is coming when no one can work. While I am in the world, I am the light of the world" (John 9:3–5).

Jesus, the light of the world, heals our blindness. He spits on the ground, makes clay with the saliva, and smears the clay on our eyes. John's Gospel recalls Genesis's story of creation and John the Baptist's story of baptism. This God of ours, ever creating us anew, then sends us to wash ourselves clean in the Pool of the Sent. Finally, we can see! The God of vision puts mud on humanity's eyes, sends humanity to wash, and gives humanity vision.

Once those who are healed of blindness begin to see, the rest of humanity, still blind, fights clear-sighted vision. The remaining saga deals with blind humanity's protest of Christ's healing gift. As Christ, the Light of the World, is persecuted and finally killed, so his disciples, healed and now able to see with Christ's own vision, will be persecuted and finally killed.

The once-blind man's neighbors and those who had seen him begging question him. "How were your eyes opened?" they ask. "The man called Jesus made clay and anointed my eyes and told me, 'Go to Siloam and wash,'" he explains. "So I went there and washed and was able to see."

They take him to the Pharisees, presumably the ones who had only hours earlier tried to stone Jesus to death. Here, in verse fourteen, we are told for the first time that Jesus heals the blind man on the Sabbath. Jesus breaks the law! And the use of spit certainly violates Jewish custom and the cleanliness laws. Jesus' healing is illegal, an act of civil disobedience. One can only wonder how the Pharisees rage against the illegal healing of Jesus on the Sabbath when, only hours earlier, they had attempted to kill Jesus—on the Sabbath!

The interrogation of the healed man turns into a courtroom drama. He takes the witness stand and faces hostile prosecutors. First, the Pharisees ask him how he can see. When he tells them, simply and truthfully, what happened, they immediately criticize Jesus. "This man is not from God because he does not keep the Sabbath." (Hours earlier they said he was not from God because he was possessed and because he claimed to be God.) There is division among them about Jesus, so they question the healed man again. "What do you have to say about him, since he opened your eyes?" The man answers, "He is a prophet." The uneducated poor person ranks Jesus among the great ancestors of Judaism—in a class with Jeremiah, Isaiah, Ezekiel, and Elijah—but his answer infuriates the authorities. Because they refuse to believe that the man was ever blind, they summon his parents and put them on trial.

"Is this your son who you say was born blind?" they ask the man's parents. "How is it that he now sees?" The parents become defensive. "We know that this is our son and that he was born blind," they declaim. "We do not know how he sees now, nor do we know who opened his eyes. Ask him. He can speak for himself." They do not defend their son. In fact, we are told, they are afraid. They know that the Judeans will expel from the synagogue anyone who acknowledges Jesus as the Messiah. Fearing excommunication and ostracizing—not wanting to get in trouble with the law—they deny any knowledge about Jesus or their son's healing. They would not, could not, risk their reputations, their social standing, or their lives for their son. They leave him alone, disappear from the story, and are never heard from again.

For a second time, the religious authorities question the once-blind man, beginning with a pious proclamation. "Give God the praise!" they acclaim, appearing holy and righteous. Yet, they have no intention of praising God; their one concern is to protect their control over the Temple, the synagogues, their religious tradition, their authority, and their privilege. "We know that this man [Jesus] is a sinner!" they declare. "If he is a sinner," the healed man testifies, "I do not know. One thing I do know is that I was blind and now I see." The man's testimony remains simple, to the point, and truthful. "What did he do to you?" they ask again. "How did he open your eyes?" "I told you already and you did not listen," the healed man replies. "Why do you want to hear it again?" he asks the sanctimonious, murderous authorities. Then he pulls all the stops: "Do you want to become his disciples, too?"

And with that, all hell breaks loose. The question holds both a confession and an invitation to discipleship to Jesus. For the first time, a disciple of Jesus challenges the authorities—something none of the other disciples in any of the Gospels ever do. The man's question is a breakthrough and, after the death and resurrection of Jesus, will eventually become the refrain of the early church.

The religious authorities go berserk. They will not stand for such an affront and immediately ridicule the man: "You are that man's disciple; we are disciples of Moses! We know that God spoke to Moses, but we do not know where this one is from." But the healed man refuses to back down. He has become the interrogator. He puts them on the stand and gives it right back to them:

> "This is what is so amazing, that you do not know where he is from, yet he opened my eyes. We know that God does not listen to sinners, but if one is devout and does his will, he listens to him. It is unheard of that anyone ever opened the eyes of a person born blind. If this man were not from God, he would not be able to do anything" (John 9:30–34).

The interrogation table has been turned around. "Who do you think you are?" they ask. "You are uneducated. You are poor. You are a complete sinner, and yet you dare to teach us?" They throw him out of the Temple.

Next to death, getting kicked out of the Temple is the worst thing that can happen to a person. One might as well be blind. It means the person is expelled from society. The once-blind man is now back to square one—no better off than when he started. He spoke the truth, defended his healer, and admitted to being a disciple of the healer. After engaging the bloodthirsty theologians and the religious authorities in debate about faith and healing, he is now completely ostracized and marginalized to the outskirts of the Temple. One presumes even his parents will have nothing to do with him.

Precisely at this moment, when he has been kicked out and ostracized and hits rock-bottom despair, Jesus appears. We are told that Jesus hears what happened to the man he healed and immediately goes looking for him. Rarely in the Gospels does Jesus go searching for anyone, even a poor person he has already helped. The story should be over. Someone has been healed, and someone was kicked out of the religious establishment by the authorities for defending Jesus. That alone marks the story as breathtaking and inspiring. But Jesus goes out on the margins looking for the man. He knows those margins well because he, too, has been kicked out of the establishment. He, too, walks alone on the edge of society.

When he finds the healed man, Jesus asks him, "Do you believe in the Son of Man?" Jesus wants to know if the once-blind man believes in him.

"Who is he, sir, that I may believe in him?" the man responds.

"You have seen him and the one speaking with you is he," Jesus answers.

"I do believe, Lord," he says as he worships Jesus. The once-blind man now sees and hears the Son of Humanity.

The discipleship journey has come full circle. After his healing, the interrogations by the religious authorities, the abandonment of his parents, and his excommunication from the Temple, the once-blind man meets Christ and worships him.

There on the margins—outside the religious establishment, in the place where those who have been kicked out of society dwell—the real journey of faith begins. Jesus seeks out the man, finds him, questions his faith, and introduces himself. When Jesus intimately reveals his true identity, the once-blind man worships Jesus as God. No disciple has ever done that before. After all he has been through—from the glorious discovery of sight to the worst possible rejection—the healed man meets God. His life is fulfilled. He has seen the Christ. He glorifies God.

While the man who was blind worships at his feet, Jesus announces:

> "I came into this world for judgment, so that those who do not see might see, and those who do see might become blind." Some of the Pharisees who were with him heard this and said to him, "Surely we

are not also blind, are we?" Jesus said to them, "If you were blind, you would have no sin; but now you are saying, 'We see,' so your sin remains" (John 9:39–41).

When Christ heals us and gives us vision, we start speaking the truth about him; we become his followers. Healing and discipleship lead to confrontation with our neighbors, the public, religious authorities, government representatives, our parents, our relatives. If we continue to speak the truth about the vision we have received from Christ, we may even be expelled from the establishment and abandoned to the margins of society. There, on the outskirts—in soup kitchens, shelters, refugee camps, hospitals, jails, prisons, and war zones, along city streets and in rough neighborhoods—Jesus seeks us out. *He comes looking for us.* He asks us if we believe in the Son of Humanity and reveals himself to us on the margins of society. Once he introduces himself to us, we worship him.

This gospel story touched me profoundly while I was in jail for my Plowshares disarmament action. After we were arrested, we endured endless questions and denunciations from soldiers, police officers, jailers, federal marshals, friends, relatives, activists, Jesuits, priests, church officials, reporters, prosecutors, FBI agents, judges, parole officers, and fellow Catholics. At times, the pressure and hostility crushed my spirit. Some days I felt so low that it seemed the only thing worse that could happen would be illness and death. Yet, in those narrow North Carolina jail cells, Christ came to us—in our Bible study, our prayer, and our daily Eucharist.

"Do you believe in the Christ?" the Scriptures ask. I had presumed that I was a disciple, that I believed in Christ, that I had already met Christ, that I had been healed, at some level, by Christ. But our action, mistrial and trials, sentencing, imprisonment, and persecution left me so shell-shocked that sometimes I was no longer sure what I knew. My suffering disoriented me. I believed, yet prayed, "Lord, help my unbelief."

Although I had long claimed the Gospel's vision, I knew then that I was blind. In the quiet hours of our daily Bible study and Eucharists, Christ reintroduced himself to me. "Where are you?" I whispered from my cell bunk. "You have seen him and the one speaking to you is he," I heard.

Inspired by this passage, I sat alone in my cell, sensing that Christ was seeking me out, that I was meeting Christ again, and that I was worshiping

Christ as never before. Perhaps in that terrible ordeal, in the fiery furnace of jail, I was learning about discipleship and worship all over again.

But I am still blind—and still on the journey. Christ is still healing me and seeking me out.

And healing and seeking each one of us.

The discipleship story continues.

chapter twenty-one

TAKE AWAY THE STONE

So Jesus, perturbed again, came to the tomb. It was a cave, and a stone lay across it. Jesus said, "Take away the stone." Martha, the dead man's sister, said to him, "Lord, by now there will be a stench; he has been dead for four days." Jesus said to her, "Did I not tell you that if you believe you will see the glory of God?" So they took away the stone. And Jesus raised his eyes and said, "Father, I thank you for hearing me. I know that you always hear me; but because of the crowd here I have said this, that they may believe that you sent me." And when he had said this, he cried out in a loud voice, "Lazarus, come out!" The dead man came out, tied hand and foot with burial bands, and his face was wrapped in a cloth. So Jesus said to them, "Untie him and let him go." (John 11:38–44)

The story of Lazarus, Martha, and Mary—a story of death and despair, life and hope—mirrors our own predicament, our own times, our own hearts. If we look carefully, we can see ourselves in every character. If we notice the rock-bottom despair in this tale, we will recognize our own despair and our own complicity in the powers of death. We will also hear the liberating voice of Jesus calling us out to new life.

The devout Judeans have just tried to kill the unarmed Jesus. Now, upon hearing the news that his dear friend Lazarus is dying and, in fact, is dead, Jesus announces that he is going to see Lazarus, which means he is going right back into the thick of things where his would-be murderers await him. This decision terrifies the disciples who fear getting killed (as we would), and so they argue with Jesus. "Don't you realize those people are trying to kill you? We can't go back there, Jesus!" they exclaim.

But notice: Jesus calls Lazarus "our friend." Lazarus is their friend, too! "What are you willing to do for your friends?" Jesus asks. "Are you willing to lay down your life for your friends? Come, let's go."

This is a story about friendship, community, and nonviolent love. For Jesus, laying down one's life for one's friends is not just a duty; it is natural. Ashamed, the disciples declare that, yes, they will go with Jesus to Bethany and beyond. "Let us go and die with him," macho Thomas asserts.

But what happens? The disciples disappear; the Twelve are nowhere to be seen in the rest of the story. Not until the next chapter do they reappear with Jesus in the desert far away from controversy.

The image we are presented with, as this episode unfolds, is one of Jesus walking alone to Bethany, back to face the crowd that just tried to kill him, there to stand with his friend. Jesus—vulnerable, unarmed, the one who values friendship more than anyone else does—walks alone.

Next, we read about the professional mourners weeping over Lazarus. These are probably the same religious people who just threatened to kill Jesus—now fulfilling their religious obligation to mourn Lazarus. They show public sorrow for his death, yet their hearts are filled with murder.

Then we meet Martha and Mary, the beloved disciples, the two heroic women who come closest to accepting Christ. They have begun the ritual thirty days of mourning and are beside themselves with grief.

Lazarus has been dead for four days. Why are we told this? According to their (Jewish) belief, the soul of the dead person leaves the body after three days. In effect, one could raise a person from the dead after two days, but after three days? Don't bother; there is nothing there. Lazarus is dead four days now, which means Lazarus is gone. Jesus is too late. There is nothing that can be done.

"Lord, if you had been here, my brother would not have died," they cry.

Such utter hopelessness sounds all too familiar. Deep down, we feel the same disappointment and faithlessness in Christ before the power of death in the world. "Lord, if you had been here," we mutter like Martha and Mary, "then perhaps so many of our relatives and friends and our sisters and brothers around the world would not have died, would not be dying. If you had been here, then perhaps death would not hold power over us. If you had been here, then perhaps we would not wage war and support injustice or hang on the nuclear brink." And the lonely, unarmed, vulnerable Jesus looks us in the eyes and says, "I am the resurrection and the life. Whoever is alive here and now, and believes in me as I walk the way of life and confront the forces of death, will never die." And he puts the question to us: "Do you believe this?"

We are told that when Jesus sees Mary and the others weeping, he is "troubled in spirit." But according to the original Greek, Jesus is not just in turmoil; he is enraged. "Where have you laid him?" he asks—and the people of the culture of death are eager to show him the tomb. They say to Jesus, "Come and see"—the same precious words of invitation that Jesus uses at the beginning of John's Gospel to welcome his friends into his new way of life. Now, the mourners seek to recruit Jesus in discipleship to the culture of death. When Jesus weeps, they shake their heads in disbelief. "If only he had done something!" This, too, sounds all too familiar. How often do we, too, shake our heads in disbelief and say, "If only he had done something."

Nobody believes in Jesus; everybody believes in death. How does this make Jesus feel? He has given his life to everyone; he comes with the gift of life; he offers every possibility for new life; he stands with the God of Life—and how is he received? He is rejected. "Hey, Jesus! Come and see our ways of death."

Jesus breaks down and weeps. As Wes Howard-Brook explains in his commentary entitled *Becoming Children of God,* contrary to everything we have been taught about this great tale, Jesus does not weep because Lazarus has died. Earlier, Jesus told us that he rejoices—he is glad—at the news of Lazarus's death. "Maybe," Jesus thinks, "just maybe, they will come to believe in me now." Instead, Jesus finds everyone given over to the control of death—and he breaks down crying. He weeps because everyone in the scene—the disciples, the religious folk, even his beloved friends Martha and Mary—everyone of them and all of us, believe not in the God of Life but in the culture of death. Jesus weeps not because his friend has died but because every drop of faith and hope has died. Similarly, all of us, like all the characters in the story, at one point or another, say: "I'm sorry, Lord. There's nothing that can be done. There is no hope. You gave it a good try, Jesus, but death does get the last word."

But the story is not over! Jesus approaches the tomb—an image that stands as one of the great moments in history. Imagine the Chinese dissident student standing before a column of tanks in Tiannamon Square; imagine

Gandhi's nonviolent followers marching toward the Dharasana Salt Mines and the soldiers with their clubs ready to strike; imagine Dr. King and the civil rights activists facing the troops, the dogs, and the fire hoses of Birmingham.

Jesus confronts death. One can almost see his mind sizing up the powers of death and concluding that if he ever has to occupy one of these chambers of death, his stay will be—brief.

There, standing before the tomb, Jesus is the God of Life. As the living God who issues the great commandments—"Thou shalt not kill!" "Beat your swords into plowshares!" and "Love your enemies!"—Jesus declares three new commandments.

First, *"Take away the stone!"*

Martha pleads with him. "Not that, Lord! No, Lord, you don't understand. There's nothing that can be done. It's been four days now. Lazarus is gone; death has won. Please don't make us confront death. Please don't trouble yourself," which means, "Please don't trouble us anymore, Jesus— even if you are the Son of God." Finally, Martha blurts out, "For God's sake, think of the stench!"

Here we have the voice of total despair, the voice of no hope whatsoever, the voice that says, "Once you're dead, you're dead!" This voice sounds all too familiar because it, too, resounds within each one of us. Martha does what we do: She resists the command to take away the stone. Why do we resist this great commandment? Because we do not want resurrection. We do not want new life. We cannot handle that much hope or that much freedom and its implications. We, too, prefer to live off the comforts of the culture of death.

But Jesus insists: *You cannot afford the luxury of despair.* Take away the stone!

So the stone is taken away and, for the first time in all eleven chapters of John's Gospel, at this climactic moment, Jesus speaks directly to God. But instead of the prayer that Martha hoped for, in which she asserts that God will grant whatever Jesus asks, Jesus does not ask God for anything. Jesus does not pray, "Please, God, raise Lazarus from the dead." He does not tell God what to do. Rather, he offers the most radical prayer of all. Before anything else happens, he simply says, "Thank you." To resist death, Jesus shows us that we have to be people of contemplative prayer, people who give thanks to the God of Life, people who trust that God hears our longings for new life.

Next, the second command, *"Lazarus, come out!"*

Lazarus represents humanity, all of us buried in the tombs of the empire of death.

"Leave your tombs!" Jesus shouts. "Come out from the power of death. Live free from the forces of death!"

Lazarus appears, but he is bound in burial clothes. He cannot hear, see, speak, reach out, or walk—actions that symbolize discipleship to Christ. Lazarus is still a victim of the culture.

And so the third command: *"Unbind him and let him go!"*

Mark's Gospel offers the command to "bind the strong man," the forces of death. Here, we have the flip side—the command to unbind the weak and let them go free.

Do the people do it? We do not know, for the story is left unfinished; Lazarus remains standing at the tomb waiting for us. Our mission today could not be clearer: Unbind humanity from the shroud of death and set it free to live in peace.

Jesus' raising of Lazarus symbolizes all the nonviolent struggles of liberation from oppression and death throughout history. It is the story of Dr. King and the civil rights movement calling forth African Americans from the tomb of racial injustice and unbinding them. It is the story of Nelson Mandela and the resisting masses ordering the stone of apartheid to be taken away—in the face of total despair—and the South African people coming forward. It is the story of Dorothy Day, A. J. Muste, and their friends refusing to take cover in fallout shelters during nuclear war air-raid drills.

It is our story, too.

In Washington, D.C., where I have lived most of my life, we are surrounded by death—from the handguns and knives on street corners; to the U.S. Congress, which contracts against the poor, votes for executions, builds new prisons, and cuts healthcare; to the Pentagon, with its preparations for war, the greatest institution for the promotion of death in the history of humanity. Death gets the last word.

And yet, and yet, in our churches, we gather in prayer; we sing; we hear the word of God; we break bread and pass the cup; we join hands with one another; we offer a sign of peace; and we go forward into the streets to say "no" to death and "yes" to life.

When my friends and I entered Seymour Johnson Air Force Base and hammered on an F15 nuclear-capable fighter bomber, in keeping with Isaiah's mandate to beat swords into plowshares, we were trying to take these commands to heart: to roll away the imperial stone of militaristic death, to call forth those entombed in the Pentagon and its military bases, and to unbind those held by the cultural trappings of death, the nuclear shroud. We were arrested, jailed, tried, and convicted—yet, I discovered, we *can* confront the powers of death. Indeed, liberation from the powers of death comes with a price, which Jesus showed with his blood on the cross. "But fear not," we are told. The God of Resurrection and Life has further plans for us. The stone will be rolled away!

Our Gospel is nothing less than a call to say "no" to the culture of death that we live in; a summons to stand against the forces of death in the Spirit of resurrection and new life; and a command to be people of hope in a land of utter despair.

Jesus commands us: "Take away the stone of death that keeps you all entombed in a culture of death. Call one another out of the tombs into new life. Unbind the dead and let them go free. Help one another out of the ties that ensnare you in the culture of death and liberate one another into the freedom of nonviolence."

We all feel the numbness of despair. "There is nothing that can be done. We will always have nuclear weapons," the culture of death convinces us. "We will always have war. We will always have violence. Death is in control, and militarism rules the land and our hearts."

Yet, the voice of Jesus rings out across the centuries with three new commandments: *Take away the stone. Come out of your tombs. Unbind the oppressed and let them go free.* In other words, Jesus summons us to stand against the culture of death and say: "No more despair. No more injustice. No more handguns. No more violence. No more death penalties. No more abortions. No more sexism. No more racism. No more homophobia. No more homelessness. No more starvation. No more consumerism. No more greed. No more contracts against the poor. No more Pentagon. No more CIA. No more Hiroshimas. No more war. No more nuclear weapons. No more big business legally profiting from systematic killing."

In other words, no more death!

As Daniel Berrigan remarked, Jesus reverses Dante and says, "Take on hope all ye who enter here."

This God of Resurrection and Life cries out to us now more than ever. "Take away the stone of death! Come out of your tombs! Unbind the dead and let them go free! You are people of resurrection and life. You are alive. Live and let live."

Hope when all hope is gone. Good news, indeed!

chapter twenty-two

TABLES OVERTURNED

They came to Jerusalem, and on entering the temple area he began to drive out those selling and buying there. He overturned the tables of the money changers and the seats of those who were selling doves. He did not permit anyone to carry anything through the temple area. Then he taught them saying, "Is it not written:

> *'My house shall be called a house of prayer for all people'?*
> *But you have made it a den of thieves."*

The chief priests and the scribes came to hear of it and were seeking a way to put him to death. (Mark 11:15–18)

Jesus loves the poor. He puts himself entirely at their service—but he does not stop there. He calls for justice and denounces the injustice of poverty—but he does not stop there either. Jesus engages in dramatic action for justice. He progresses from doing the good works of charity to speaking out for justice to taking risks through direct, public action against injustice. Eventually, of course, his journey leads him into conflict with the unjust status quo—confrontation is inevitable. In fact, he seeks it.

Gandhi called Jesus the "most active nonviolent resister known to history." Like Gandhi marching to the sea to make salt, and Dr. King walking illegally through Birmingham's downtown park to protest segregation, Jesus wages a public campaign of peaceful revolution from Galilee to Jerusalem where, according to all four Gospels, he disrupts business as usual in the Temple, the center of Jewish life. He practices nonviolent civil disobedience by driving out those who bought and sold, by turning over the tables of the money changers and the seats of the dove sellers, by refusing to permit anyone to carry anything through the Temple, and by calling for prayer instead of commerce. He decries those who turned God's house into a shopping mall. Risking his life, he cries out, "You have made it a den of robbers." According to the synoptic Gospels, this outburst leads immediately to his arrest, jailing, trial, torture, and execution.

Why does Jesus risk everything in the Temple? Because the Temple system complements the Roman Empire's economic oppression of the people. It epitomizes religious-based, institutional injustice. It robs the poor in God's name—those who are taught by their own religious authorities that God dwells only in the Temple and that pilgrimages and large financial contributions are required for legitimate worship. While blessing the Roman Empire, the Temple system gives economic, ideological, and political power to the religious authorities. Thus God's house becomes, as Jeremiah described it centuries earlier, "a den of thieves."

The Temple is an expensive, religious Disneyland. Each year, eighteen thousand lambs are slaughtered in the Temple at the time of Passover. The population of Jerusalem quadruples, and the faithful are required to pay a hefty Temple tax. At the height of Passover, the Temple operates as the "national bank," offering loans, keeping track of debts, and changing money so that the Temple tax can be paid. The poor, especially women, the ill, and other outcasts, have to purchase expensive doves so they can be "purified" and made "worthy" to worship on the fringe of the Temple.

Jesus confronts this unjust structure head on. As Ched Myers observes, Jesus does not merely want lower prices for the poor, and he does not seek to reform the Temple. Rather, he overturns the tables and calls for its complete transformation. He demands an end to the entire cultic system. Forbidding people to carry any goods in or out of the house of prayer, Jesus shuts down Temple operations altogether. From that point on, he announces, God can be found within every human heart, within every faith-filled, forgiving community. This teaching terrifies, threatens, and outrages the chief priests, the Pharisees, and the scribes because they know that if it is accepted, they will lose their economic and political privilege.

The action in the Temple is the culmination of Jesus' lifelong obedience to God and civil disobedience to imperial and religious injustice. Jesus has engaged in many types of civil disobedience before this scene, but this event makes the boldest political statement in the entire Bible.

Jesus' action is perfectly nonviolent. He does not hurt anyone; he does not use violence against anyone; he does not kill anyone; and he does not take a whip against anyone. As always, Jesus is neither passive nor silent. Rather, he is provocative and daring.

Jesus does not just criticize the Temple's economic oppression of the poor: He pleads for its restoration as a house of prayer. In later verses, he instructs his disciples to worship God in the realm of faith, through forgiveness and community. While liberating the oppressed from institutionalized injustice, Jesus focuses his ultimate attention—and ours—on God. The point of the action is an urgent call for true worship, honest prayer, and right relationship with God.

This story summons us to engage in nonviolent direct action against injustice and in contemplative praise of God. While the Church calls people to the life of prayer, it rarely invokes the civilly disobedient Jesus who overturns tables and drives out the buyers and sellers. Perhaps we fear the implications of this story. How would Jesus respond today to the many institutions that oppress the world's poor, beginning with the Pentagon, the U.S. Congress, Wall Street corporations, the Department of Energy, the S.A.C. Base, or the Trident submarine bases? Surely Jesus would be as active and dramatic in his resistance to such unjust institutions. He would expect bold, public acts from his followers, regardless of the legal consequences.

The scene in the Temple makes me feel afraid and anxious. Knowing that his actions lead to his arrest and crucifixion, I tremble as I imagine it and reflect on its meaning for my own discipleship. My Plowshares disarmament action was an attempt to walk in the footsteps of the civilly disobedient Jesus. I hammered on a nuclear-capable fighter bomber not only to call for disarmament but to side with the troublemaking, provocative Jesus. This gospel story and others push me to confront my fears and to try to act as Jesus would act in the face of such crimes. Our Plowshares action was frightening yet also grace-filled. The action and the days in jail that followed were deeply contemplative—and I hope they will bear good fruit for peace. Such acts of resistance need to occur wherever injustice and war threaten humanity. In this way, we manifest our faith in our illegal, antiwar, civilly disobedient God. I know such acts will continue to happen wherever Christians live.

And I know, too, that I need not fear. The ultimate focus of Jesus' action is his call for contemplative prayer and true worship. I can be grateful that Jesus stands up for justice, for the poor, and for God, and can rejoice in this call to prayer. I need not fear if I take time each day to enter into the house of prayer, beginning in the solitude of my own heart—there to worship God with gratitude and love. Finally, this dramatic story takes away my fears and leads me from the house of prayer into the life of active nonviolence to help transform the world into God's house of peace.

chapter twenty-three

WASH EACH OTHER'S FEET

[Jesus] rose from supper and took off his outer garments. He took a towel and tied it around his waist. Then he poured water into a basin and began to wash the disciples' feet and dry them with the towel around his waist. He came to Simon Peter, who said to him, "Master, are you going to wash my feet?" Jesus answered and said to him, "What I am doing, you do not understand now, but you will understand later." Peter said to him, "You will never wash my feet." Jesus answered him, "Unless I wash you, you will have no inheritance with me." Simon Peter said to him, "Master, then not only my feet, but my hands and head as well." Jesus said to him, "Whoever has bathed has no need except to have his feet washed, for he is clean all over; so you are clean, but not all." For he knew who would betray him; for this reason, he said, "Not all of you are clean."

So when he had washed their feet (and) put his garments back on and reclined at table again, he said to them, "Do you realize what I have done for you? You call me 'teacher' and 'master,' and rightly so, for indeed I am. If I, therefore, the master and teacher, have washed your feet, you ought to wash one another's feet. I have given you a model to follow, so that as I have done for you, you should also do. Amen, amen, I say to you, no slave is greater than his master nor any messenger greater than the one who sent him. If you understand this, blessed are you if you do it."
(John 13:4–17)

During my eight months in jail for our antinuclear action, I shared a small cell with longtime peacemaker Philip Berrigan. We were kept indoors in our cells the entire time. A small room connected our cell to another cell where our friend Bruce Friedrich was held. Each day, Phil, Bruce, and I spent several hours discussing the Scriptures. After nearly eight months—by the time of our sentencing—we had studied the entire Gospel of Mark and had discussed half of the Gospel of John.

On our last day together, before I was to be released that evening at midnight, the three of us opened our Gospel to the story of Jesus washing his disciples' feet. As we read the passage, we began to understand this story not so much as a call to serve one another by literally washing one another's feet but as a call to prepare one another for martyrdom. We recalled the previous chapter in John's Gospel when, six days before the Last Supper, Jesus attends a party in his honor at the home of his friends, Mary, Martha, and Lazarus in Bethany, just outside of Jerusalem. When Mary takes a pound of costly perfume made of pure nard, we read, anoints Jesus' feet, and wipes them with her hair, the house is filled with the fragrance of the perfume. But Judas chastises her, asking, "Why was this perfume not sold for three hundred days' wages and the money given to the poor?" Judas does not care about the poor, the Evangelist writes. Rather, he keeps the common purse and steals from it. "Leave her alone," Jesus says. "She bought it so that she might keep it for the day of my burial. You always have the poor with you, but you do not always have me" (see John 12:1–9).

"Leave her alone." Finally, Jesus finds someone among his friends who understands and supports his journey to the cross. He has been telling his disciples that he must suffer and die, that they must carry their own crosses, and that death is the doorway to resurrection. Although the (male) disciples will have none of it, Mary of Bethany purchases perfume and anoints Jesus in anticipation of his death. She accepts Jesus' destiny, and Jesus is consoled by her loving response. Here is a true disciple, someone who affirms him in his hour of need.

Then, a few verses later, we read that Jesus washes the feet of his disciples. In jail, we concluded that Mary of Bethany's anointing of Jesus inspired him to wash his disciples' feet. Why would he wash their feet? To prepare them for their own death just as Mary had prepared him. After he washes their feet, he asks them if they understand what he has done. They do not, but Jesus knows that later on, when they face martyrdom, they will.

The Evangelist uses specific verbs to describe the scene. As Wes Howard-Brook writes in his commentary titled *Becoming Children of God,* these verbs occur in John's Gospel only in the crucifixion and resurrection accounts. "He rose from supper," we are told. As the early community would have known, we recognize that this is the risen Lord acting. "He took off his outer garment. He took a towel and tied it around his waist." These verbs appear later in John's description of the crucifixion, and later in the teaching to Peter that "someone will tie a belt around your waist and lead you where you would rather not go." And then, "He poured water into a basin and began to wash the disciples' feet and dry them with the towel around his waist."

These loaded verbs describe the paschal mystery of Jesus and, in the context of this story, they take on new significance. Jesus prepares his disciples not only to walk with him as he undergoes his crucifixion and resurrection, but to undergo their own crucifixion by the empire and eventual resurrection by God:

> When he had washed their feet (and) put his garments back on and reclined at table again, he said to them, "Do you realize what I have done for you? You call me 'teacher' and 'master,' and rightly so, for indeed I am. If I, therefore, the master and teacher, have washed your feet, you ought to wash one another's feet. I have given you a model to follow, so that as I have done for you, you should also do. Amen, amen, I say to you, no slave is greater than his master nor any messenger greater than the one who sent him. If you understand this, blessed are you if you do it." (John 13:12–17)

Do you realize what I have done for you? he asks them.

They do not. Yet, he has given them a way to help one another face the inevitable suffering that lies ahead. His community of followers must prepare one another not only to walk the way of nonviolence but to undergo the violence and death that the principalities and powers inflict. Now, with the encouraging support of one's community members, one can face imprisonment, suffering, and martyrdom.

Do you realize what I have done for you? Jesus asks. *I have prepared you for death. I am showing you how to prepare one another for death. By helping one another, serving one another, anointing one another, and loving one another as I have loved you, you will be ready to take up your cross, die, and rise. On that day, you will understand what I have done for you.*

Eventually, when they become a community of martyrs, they understand. They teach one another to resist the empire nonviolently, to cling to their faith in Christ, and to walk to their deaths without fear.

If studied in this way, this famous Scripture passage offers people of faith around the world a way to prepare one another to face death. The story invites us to strengthen one another as Mary of Bethany strengthens Jesus and Jesus strengthens his friends. This act encourages us to take up the cross of nonviolent resistance to evil. Emboldened by our sisters and brothers, we can face the police, the jails, the trials, the torture, and the forces of death that the world would inflict.

When we wash one another's feet, we anoint one another and help one another walk to our deaths. We prepare one another to undergo the cross and resurrection. We are made ready to follow our Lord into death and eternal life.

chapter twenty-four

REMAIN IN ME

"Do not let your hearts be troubled. You have faith in God; have faith also in me . . . [W]hoever believes in me will do the works that I do, and will do greater ones than these, because I am going to the Father . . . If you ask anything of me in my name, I will do it. If you love me, you will keep my commandments. . . . On that day you will realize that I am in my Father and you are in me and I in you. Whoever has my commandments and observes them is the one who loves me. And whoever loves me will be loved by my Father, and I will love [them] and reveal myself to [them]. . . . Whoever loves me will keep my word, and my Father will love [them], and we will come to [them] and make our dwelling with [them] . . . Peace I leave with you; my peace I give to you. Not as the world gives do I give it to you. Do not let your hearts be troubled or afraid. . . . Remain in me, as I remain in you. . . . Whoever remains in me and I in [them] will bear much fruit, because without me you can do nothing. . . . If you remain in me and my words remain in you, ask for whatever you want and it will be done for you. . . . As the Father loves me, so I also love you. Remain in my love. If you keep my commandments, you will remain in my love, just as I have kept my Father's commandments and remain in his love. I have told you this so that my joy may be in you and your joy may be complete. This is my commandment: love one another as I love you. No one has greater love than this, to lay down one's life for one's friends. You are my friends if you do what I command you. (John 14:1, 12, 14–15, 20, 23, 27; 15:4–5, 7, 9–14)

While challenging the structures of injustice and strengthening us to face death on the cross, Jesus also invites us to intimacy with God. Halfway through John's revolutionary story comes a loving plea to enter into the fullness of God's own life. The words are urgent, vulnerable, political, and promising: "Do not be troubled. Have faith in me. Remain in me. Share my peace, my joy, my love."

How do we "remain in Jesus"? The Gospel urges us to keep his words and obey his commandments, words and commandments that are narrowed down to a simple plea for love: "Love one another as I love you, as I have given my life for you." Obedience to his word of love leads us into God's house of love, into the heart of Jesus.

Remaining in Jesus requires that we center ourselves in his presence through daily contemplative prayer. Saint Ignatius Loyola, founder of the Society of Jesus, taught a spirituality centered in the life of Jesus. He recommends that each day we withdraw into quiet solitude and enter into the intimate love of God the creator, Jesus, and their Spirit. We begin this prayer by asking God to help us to be open, receptive, listening, and attentive to God's presence. Then, as we contemplate Jesus by imagining a scene from the Gospels, we enter the story and become part of Jesus' own story. As we look at Jesus, listen to his words, and feel his spirit upon us, we are transformed; we live in his presence. We attend to his life-giving word and know his peace, joy, and love. We can go forward into the world alive in his presence, filled with his peace, offering his love to all, radiating his complete joy.

The Gospel portrays a vulnerable Jesus who longs for us to live his life. By entering into his story through daily contemplative prayer, we grow in the subtleties of his consoling peace. Because we continually resist God's presence within us and in the world, we need to return each day to that intimate place with God so that we can remain in God's peace. Over time, we remain in Jesus.

As a Jesuit, I struggle to take quality time in prayer to remain in Christ. I sit in silence, read a Scripture passage, and dwell in the presence of Christ—and nothing dramatic happens. Yet, each time I do this I can almost feel Christ in my prayer say, "I love you, I am with you, I want you to be with me." Afterwards I feel transformed and reenergized, and my day takes on new meaning because now it is rooted in Christ's love.

The Gospel presumes that we have already met Christ. It challenges us to *remain* in him—a beautiful yet difficult invitation. As an unfaithful disciple, a sinner, I continually repent of the many ways I reject Christ, and I struggle daily to remain in Christ. Daily prayer, Eucharist, spiritual direction, Bible study, the sacraments, and the wider Church help me to remain in Christ. But community life offers one of the most crucial ways to remain in Christ. By building community with other Christians, even living with them, our relationship to Christ deepens. For over fifteen years, I have lived in community, sharing every aspect of my life with other Jesuits in small, intentional, inner-city communities, and large, institutional communities all over the country. Over the years, community life has brought much pain, deep disappointment, terrible frustration, and humiliation. But more than that, it has offered moments of sheer joy, deep peace, and profound communion with God and others. On the whole, I do not think I could continue the struggle to live in and remain in Christ without community support.

As I write this, I live in a Jesuit community in Manhattan. Most of our twenty-three community members have lived in this community for at least fifteen years, and each member is engaged in a different apostolic work. Some teach university or high school students; some work directly with the homeless; some serve as chaplains to the dying; some minister to the gay and lesbian community; some do administrative work; some work full-time on issues of peace and justice. One member is a full-time spiritual director and massage therapist. Together, we live in an old apartment building on the edge of Harlem. Some of us share apartments, and a few have their own studio apartments. Each evening we share Eucharist and a common meal.

Several times a year, we go away for days of prayer, reflection, and relaxation. On a recent weekend, our community traveled to a house in the country where we spent the initial Friday night sitting informally in a living room, telling stories, laughing at jokes, and enjoying one another's company. The next morning we broke into small groups for reflection on our apostolic mission. For over two hours we discussed questions about justice, solidarity with the poor, disarmament, education, and healthcare. Later, in the afternoon, we gathered in a circle to listen to one another speak about our respective lives, work, interests, and pain; we shared our brokenness. Then we read from the Scriptures and shared the body and blood of Christ, and the evening concluded with a delicious meal that lasted long into the night. Our weekend away took us deep into one another's lives and thus into the life of Christ. We felt Christ present in our midst, especially during the liturgy. Over the years, these gatherings help us remain in Jesus. Contemplative prayer and community life keep us focused on Jesus over the long haul.

But the Gospels do not promote a "new age spirituality" that permits us to ask, "What's in it for me?" The focus of the Gospel, in fact, is never on the self but on Christ. Even personal prayer is complemented not only by community life but by public activity with Christ in the world. To remain in Christ, we serve Christ in the world, in the poor, in our enemies, in the marginalized, and in the struggle for justice, disarmament, and peace.

Christ is political. His politics of nonviolence lead to his death. To remain in him is to take sides in the world, to side with the poor and the marginalized, to work with those who seek God's reign of peace and justice. To remain in Christ, we remain among the poor. We remain in the struggle for justice and peace. We remain in pursuit of disarmament, whether or not it is popular, whether or not we are successful. We pursue nonviolence because we remain in Christ. This is our life; we are Christ's. We have been chosen by Christ and we continually choose to remain in Christ.

A few hours before his arrest, Jesus issues this plea to remain in him. Knowing that his friends will abandon him, he invites them to remain in him beyond word and deed: He offers them his body and blood, the Eucharist.

chapter twenty-five

BROKEN BREAD, BLOOD SHED

When the hour came, he took his place at table with the apostles. He said to them, "I have eagerly desired to eat this Passover with you before I suffer, for, I tell you, I shall not eat it (again) until there is fulfillment in the kingdom of God." Then he took a cup, gave thanks, and said, "Take this and share it among yourselves; for I tell you (that) from this time on I shall not drink of the fruit of the vine until the kingdom of God comes." Then he took the bread, said the blessing, broke it, and gave it to them, saying, "This is my body, which will be given for you; do this in memory of me." And likewise the cup after they had eaten, saying, "This cup is the new covenant in my blood, which will be shed for you." (Luke 22:14–20)

While I was in jail, I received thousands of letters of support. Many people thanked us for our disarmament witness, offered us their prayers, and shared their own struggle with nonviolence. But I also received painful letters from relatives and friends, especially friends within the peace movement who were angry with me. They opposed our action and refused to support us. Several friendships ruptured, in fact, and I felt hurt.

Each day, Phil, Bruce, and I shared Eucharist together in our small cell. We spent several hours in Bible study, then broke a piece of Wonder bread and passed a small cup of grape juice, which we had saved for our offering. During Holy Week, when we spent many hours reflecting on the meaning of Eucharist, I wondered how Jesus felt when his friends rejected him and how he responded to their rejection of him.

The Last Supper occurs one or two days after Jesus' civil disobedience in the Temple, perhaps shortly after his raising of Lazarus. Even as the authorities plot his arrest and execution, Jesus knows his days—even his hours—are numbered. According to John's Gospel, at that crisis moment during the Last Supper, Jesus tells his disciples that he no longer calls them "servants" or "slaves"; rather, he calls them his "friends." He looks into their eyes, sees their fear, and knows that they do not believe in him. He can tell that at any minute they will run from him, betray him, deny him, abandon him. As Jesus reflects on his friendship and love for them, and their impending rejection of him, he reaches out even further in a gesture of intimate love. He offers himself completely to them in the hope that his friends might accept him and stay with him. He tells them that he wants to be their food and drink—that he is giving them his body and blood. We can imagine their reaction: They do not know what he is talking about. Perhaps they think he is crazy. Ultimately, as we know, everyone rejects him and his way of the cross. Yet, Jesus loves his friends further—to the point of becoming their food and drink.

In the Eucharist, he offers himself to us so that we can share in his intimate life with God. He wants to reconcile us and deepen our friendship with him and God. When I felt abandoned and rejected by some of my friends while I was in jail, I was tempted to retaliate by cutting myself off from them. Then I realized that in far worse circumstances, Jesus responds to rejection by making himself even more vulnerable and reaching out even more completely with friendship and love.

The Eucharist is a sharing in friendship and love with Christ. It reconciles all of us in his body and blood. We accept him as our food and drink—our very life blood. We enter into intimacy with Jesus and, in the process, share human intimacy with all those gathered around the Lord's table. As we grow in friendship and love with those around us, we remember the life of Jesus. He comes alive in our memory—just as he had hoped. He becomes present to us here and now, and we become present to one another. He becomes the peace between us, and we are transformed.

On one weekend away, my Jesuit community shared an especially profound experience of Eucharist. We had spent the day talking and listening to one another about our Jesuit mission and our personal struggles. That evening, we began our liturgy without words; together, we hummed the Buddhist mantra, "Ohmm." After several minutes of sounding this mantra on a strong, vibrating note, and entering into a sacred, quiet space, we read from the Scriptures. For our intercessory prayer, we lifted up the names of those who had died, those we love, those who persecute us, and those in need. Hundreds of people were invoked, and our circle widened with each name. The presider then invited a community member from the circle to kneel with him at the low table in the center of the room and recite the Eucharistic Prayer. Because there was no Sacramentary and no written prayer, the other Jesuit said with a panic, "I don't remember the words." "Do it anyway," the presider insisted. So he picked up the bread and said, "This is my body," and he lifted up the cup filled with wine and said, "This is my blood. Whenever you do this, remember me." Then he returned to his chair. Stunned by the stark, simple words, we stood, joined hands, recited the Lord's Prayer, embraced one another with Christ's peace, and shared communion.

At that Eucharist, we experienced the Lord's presence in our midst. We felt like Zen students who are struck on the back with a bamboo reed by our master. For a moment, we awoke with a shock to the spiritual truth of reality: We re-membered Christ—and we left that retreat with a deeper awareness of our common friendship in Christ.

At the moment of betrayal, denial, fear, and abandonment, Jesus makes himself more vulnerable and offers himself to his friends—and how do they respond? According to Luke's account, Jesus follows the gift of his body and blood by announcing that one of them will betray him. The disciples debate "who among them would do such a deed. Then an argument broke out among them about which of them should be regarded as the greatest" (Luke 22:23–24). In response to his gift, the disciples discuss how great they themselves are! Jesus reprimands them:

> The kings of the Gentiles lord it over them and those in authority over them are addressed as 'Benefactors'; but among you it shall not be so. Rather, let the greatest among you be as the youngest, and the leader as the servant . . . I am among you as the one who serves (Luke 22:25–27).

Then Jesus tells his friend Peter that he has prayed for him. "Once you have turned back, you must strengthen your brothers," he says (Luke 22:32). Although Peter pledges to go to prison and die with Jesus, Jesus sees Peter's doubts and fears and knows that within a few hours Peter will deny knowing him three times.

As we enter deeply into communion with the Lord, we touch our basic humanity—both the blessing of friendship and love, and the curse of ambition, denial, and betrayal. With each Eucharist we face the choice to receive Christ's word with love or to assert ourselves and our own ambitions and pave the way for our ongoing rejection, denial, and betrayal of Christ. Real Eucharist is a quiet, hidden sharing in the paschal mystery of Christ, in his death and resurrection. As we share his body and blood, we enter into his life where we join ourselves with his journey of peace, from the works of mercy and healing to the works of justice and peace and, finally, to his work of nonviolence—his death and resurrection. Remembering Jesus—partaking in his body and blood—demands an ethical change in our lives. With each Eucharist, we deepen our sharing in Christ's ongoing transformation of the world, in his mission to proclaim God's reign of justice and peace with our lives.

Archbishop Oscar Romero spent his last three years speaking out publicly for justice and peace, calling for an end to the killing and injustice in El Salvador. Each Sunday he presided at a eucharistic celebration in San Salvador's cathedral while his homilies were broadcast to every village around the country. He denounced that week's murders committed by the military and issued Christ's call to conversion, peace, and justice. As the death threats against him increased, he told his friends that he would rise in the Salvadoran people. On March 23, 1980, he preached from the cathedral pulpit an open call to the Salvadoran military, telling them not to obey an order to kill but to obey Christ's order to serve others and bring true justice. "No soldier is obliged to obey an order against the law of God," he declared. "No one has to fulfill an immoral law. In the name of God and in the name of this suffering people, whose laments rise to heaven each day more tumultuous, I beg you, I beseech you, I order you in the name of God, stop the repression!"[1]

The next afternoon Romero celebrated a quiet liturgy in honor of a friend who had died the year before. Seconds after he concluded his homily, as he stood at the altar with a huge crucifix behind him, he was shot and killed. His last words and the example of his martyrdom explain the meaning of Christ's eucharistic gift:

You have just heard in Christ's Gospel that one must not love oneself so much as to avoid getting involved in the risks of life that history demands of us, and that those who try to fend off the danger will lose their lives. But whoever out of love for Christ give themselves to the service of others will live, like the grain of wheat that dies, but only apparently. If it did not die, it would remain alone. The harvest comes about only because it dies, allowing itself to be sacrificed in the earth and destroyed. Only by undoing itself does it produce the harvest. . . . Every effort to better society, especially when injustice and sin are so ingrained, is an effort that God blesses, that God wants, that God demands of us. . . . Dear brothers and sisters, let us all view these matters at this historic moment with that hope, that spirit of giving and sacrifice. Let us all do what we can. We can all do something. . . . This Eucharist is an act of faith. With Christian faith we know that at this moment the bread is changed into the body of the Lord, who offered himself for the world's redemption, and in this cup, the wine is transformed into the blood that was the price of salvation. May this body immolated and this blood sacrificed for humans nourish us also, so that we may give our body and blood to suffering and to pain—like Christ, not for self, but to teach justice and peace to our people. So let us join together intimately in faith and hope at this moment of prayer.[2]

When Jesus offers his body and blood to us, he speaks of a renewal of the covenant and calls it the "blood of the covenant." Like Romero, we are invited to sit at the Lord's table, eat his body, drink his blood, share in his life, and accept our side of the new covenant in Christ's blood. To be keepers of the covenant of Christ's blood, we, too, have to give our bodies, our blood, our hearts, our lives, for one another and humanity.

Like Jesus, Romero, and the martyrs, we prefer to shed our own blood for others, rather than shed the blood of others. We prefer to accept suffering rather than inflict suffering on others. We prefer to take up the cross rather than put others on the cross. We prefer to die rather than to kill.

From now on, we commit ourselves to God's reign coming to earth here and now, to that day when no more bodies will be broken and no more blood will be shed. From now on, we are keepers of the covenant of nonviolence.

chapter twenty-six

GETHSEMANE

Then they came to a place named Gethsemane, and he said to his disciples, "Sit here while I pray." He took with him Peter, James, and John, and began to be troubled and distressed. Then he said to them, "My soul is sorrowful even to death. Remain here and keep watch." He advanced a little and fell to the ground and prayed that if it were possible the hour might pass by him; he said, "Abba, Father, all things are possible to you. Take this cup away from me, but not what I will but what you will." When he returned he found them asleep. He said to Peter, "Simon, are you asleep? Could you not keep watch for one hour? Watch and pray that you may not undergo the test. The spirit is willing but the flesh is weak." Withdrawing again, he prayed, saying the same thing. Then he returned once more and found them asleep, for they could not keep their eyes open and did not know what to answer him. He returned a third time and said to them, "Are you still sleeping and taking your rest? It is enough. The hour has come. Behold, the Son of Man is to be handed over to sinners. Get up, let us go. See, my betrayer is at hand. (Mark 14:32–42)

The Gospel gives few descriptions of Jesus at prayer. We know, of course, that he prays for forty days in the desert, that he sometimes goes off alone to pray in an isolated place, and that he prays with his friends on a mountaintop. Before he appoints his twelve chosen disciples, he spends an entire night absorbed in prayer.

But the scene in the Garden of Gethsemane reveals more than a gift for quiet meditation. The Gospels portray Jesus, prior to his arrest and execution, praying in a state of sheer terror. Mark's Gospel speaks of "great trouble and distress" (see 14:33); Matthew notes that Jesus feels "sorrow and distress" (26:37); Luke records, "He was in such agony and he prayed so fervently that his sweat became like drops of blood falling on the ground" (22:44).

What is Jesus' prayer? That he might not be arrested and killed! All along Jesus moves like a living icon of courage and faith, instructing people to take up the cross. But here we find an all-too-human Jesus begging God to "take this cup away," but with the crucial caveat, "yet not as I will but as you will."

Who of us has prayed with such intensity? Who can understand what our Savior went through? This is the prayer of those who hit rock bottom, the prayer of fear, grief, and doubt that confronts us before death. This is the prayer of the martyrs.

We know that at the moment of arrest, throughout his trial and torture, and until his dying breath, Jesus remains faithful and loving. How can he—or anyone—stay so centered in faith, so nonviolent? The answer is because he prays so intensely in the garden beforehand. He has wrestled with his situation, brought his desires before God, and received an inner peace through that prayerful agony. We know this because, as Luke tells us, God sends an angel to strengthen and comfort Jesus (see Luke 22:43). Perhaps the angel's sudden appearance gives Jesus new resolve to go forward, determined to face death with dignity, faith, and forgiveness. Certainly Jesus knows that his prayer is heard. God respects Jesus' wish that ultimately God's will be done.

"Sit here while I pray," Jesus tells Peter, James, and John. "My soul is sorrowful even unto death. Remain here and keep watch." The Gospel urges us to sit with Jesus as he prays. (The heartbreak of Psalm 42 is invoked.) In this final scene, Jesus reveals the inner depths of his life. He tells us that his soul is sorrowful unto death for he has become, as the iconographers later depict him, "the man of sorrows."

This is not a comforting, detached Jesus. Rather, he is torn apart and begs his friends to stay with him. "Sit here. Remain here. Keep watch." Even though he had earlier foreseen that they would flee from him, he still needs his friends to help him get through this dark night of the soul. But who can remain with such intense sorrow? Certainly not the disciples; they fall asleep.

We cannot condemn the disciples, however, for most of us also rest comfortably while Christ's agony continues today in the plight of the poor. Like the disciples, we cannot handle anyone who so wholeheartedly enters the pain of reality and stays there, fully present. We prefer to avoid pain at all costs, and so we sleep tight while others undergo the empire's terrors. Mark describes the prayer in detail:

> He advanced a little and fell to the ground and prayed that if it were possible the hour might pass by him; he said, "Abba, Father, all things are possible to you. Take this cup away from me, but not what I will but what you will" (Mark 14:35–36).

Jesus falls to the ground, in total supplication and humiliation, and addresses God intimately, as a terrified child to a loving parent. This scene is the only episode in which Mark uses the term *Abba* for God. He affirms God's power to do anything God wants. Jesus orders God, "Take this cup away from me," while insisting that God's will be done.

When he returns to the disciples, Jesus finds them asleep. As at the moment of his glory, the Transfiguration, the disciples sleep through Jesus' most intense and personal crisis. "Simon, are you asleep?" Jesus asks. "Could you not keep watch for one hour?" Jesus has been praying in agony on the ground for an entire hour, and his one request—that his friends sit attentively nearby to support him—has not been honored. They cannot keep watch. Perhaps he wants them to be on the lookout for Judas and the arresting soldiers so that they can slip away to safety. At dinner, a few hours earlier, they argued about who among them was the greatest. At that time, Peter bragged that he would go to jail and die for Jesus. Yet, here they are—asleep! Jesus pointedly reverts to calling Peter "Simon," his pre-discipleship name for, in Jesus' eyes, Peter is no longer his disciple.

"Watch and pray." Jesus' Gethsemane request to the disciples lingers through the centuries as an invitation to contemplate Christ's intercession before God. With these simple words, the Gospels summarize the Christian task in the world: We sit with Christ in the garden, remain with Christ in his agony, keep watch with Christ as he awaits his arrest and crucifixion. We pray with Christ. As Christians, we are nonviolent contemplatives who watch over the world's injustice and hold vigil with Christ in a prayer that injustice will cease. Yet, who among us faithfully lives the contemplative life of watching and praying? Like the disciples, our spirit may be willing but our flesh is all too weak.

Jesus returns to his prayer of agony and then comes back a second time to find the disciples asleep. "They could not keep their eyes open,"

Mark writes, "and did not know what to answer him" (14:40). The disciples are dumbstruck, unable to speak the truth, afraid to repent and apologize to Jesus. They cannot say the obvious: "Yes, Jesus, we fell asleep. We are sorry. We have let you down one more time. Forgive us. We want to stay with you, to support you in this time of need, and to remain awake and keep watch with you. Help us to support you."

The Gospels highlight the blindness of not only humanity in general but the disciples in particular. Only Bartimaeus, in Mark's Gospel, and the once-blind disciple, in John's Gospel, accept the vision Jesus offers. The disciples in Gethsemane, however, "could not keep their eyes open." The phrase characterizes the lethargy and apathy of today's somnolent Church. We cannot see because we keep falling asleep, even though Christ is in agony a few feet in front of us.

A third time Jesus returns to find his friends sleeping. "Are you still sleeping and taking your rest?" he asks. "It is enough. The hour has come." He goes on to say that the Son of Humanity "is to be handed over to sinners. Get up, let us go. See, my betrayer is at hand." Now we know why he wants the disciples—and us—to watch: His betrayer approaches. Jesus wants us to see the injustice that is happening; he wants us to keep our eyes wide open. The command could not be simpler, clearer, or bolder: See!

As we enter into the story and try to obey Christ's commands to see, to stay awake, to keep watch, and to pray, we understand Gethsemane as an image of the world. Everywhere around us the forces of death arrest and capture the forces of life. In the midst of this violent world, Christ keeps watch and prays. Interceding on our behalf, he maintains his spirit of nonviolence to the end. He asks us to stay at his side, to watch with him, and to pray that we and the human race may not be put to the test, that we may remain nonviolent. Within and through the struggle of prayer, Jesus faces the demons of doubt and despair and goes forward to confront the demonic powers of imperial violence. He would have us learn from him and join him in his divine mission of nonviolent transformation.

Alas for him—and for ourselves. We do wake up, but just when he needs support, we scatter to the four winds.

chapter twenty-seven

JESUS' LAST WORDS:
"PUT YOUR SWORD BACK!"

> *While he was still speaking, Judas, one of the Twelve, arrived, accompanied by a large crowd, with swords and clubs, who had come from the chief priests and the elders of the people. His betrayer had arranged a sign with them, saying, "The man I shall kiss is the one; arrest him." Immediately he went over to Jesus and said, "Hail, Rabbi!" and he kissed him. Jesus answered him, "Friend, do what you have come for." Then stepping forward they laid hands on Jesus and arrested him. And behold, one of those who accompanied Jesus put his hand to his sword, drew it, and struck the high priest's servant, cutting off his ear. Then Jesus said to him, "Put your sword back into its sheath, for all who take the sword will perish by the sword. Do you think that I cannot call upon my Father and he will not provide me at this moment with more than twelve legions of angels? But then how would the scriptures be fulfilled which say that it must come to pass in this way?" At that hour Jesus said to the crowds, "Have you come out as against a robber, with swords and clubs to seize me? Day after day I sat teaching in the temple area, yet you did not arrest me. But all this has come to pass that the writings of the prophets may be fulfilled." Then all the disciples left him and fled. (Matthew 26:47–56)*

Jesus is betrayed by one of his closest friends. The four Gospels reverberate with shock as Christ is handed over to the authorities by someone from his own inner circle. Once he is handed over to the soldiers, however, all the disciples abandon him; the betrayal spreads like a contagion. At that catastrophic moment, the unarmed Jesus calls out one last plea for nonviolence—and his cry still echoes through the centuries, waiting to be heard.

Judas arrives with a "large crowd, with swords and clubs, who had come from the chief priests and the elders of the people." Obviously, the authorities expect violence from the Jesus community. They come at night with "lanterns, torches, and weapons" (John 18:3), ready for a surprise capture. Judas then identifies Jesus, who would not have looked any different in appearance from the other Galilean fishermen, by kissing him. One presumes that the "kiss of peace" was the common, intimate greeting used by Jesus and the early community. Judas mocks Jesus, as if he were the emperor. "Hail, rabbi!" he exclaims. Jesus responds more humanly: He calls Judas "friend." "Do what you have come for," he tells his friend.

Judas is notable not only because he holds the community purse and steals from it (see John 12:6), but because he compromises with the political, religious, and imperial authorities. When he asks the chief priest "What are you willing to give me if I hand him over to you?" we are told that they "paid him thirty pieces of silver, and from that time on he looked for an opportunity to hand him over" (Matthew 26:15–16).

Judas holds no allegiance to Jesus. In fact, the Evangelists state flatly that "Satan entered him" (John 13:27), "Satan" being a frequently used code name for the demonic spirit of the empire. Perhaps Judas falls prey to the lure of power that the chief priests have. Perhaps he just wants the money. In the end, Judas, like many betraying Christians since then, worships mammon not God, and hands Christ over to the forces of death for his own personal profit. In the end, although Jesus forgives him, loves him, and continues to call him friend, Judas' love for money lures him into the demonic spirit of destruction. He spirals out of control until he kills himself.

The soldiers and the authorities "laid hands" on Jesus and arrest him. At that moment of confrontation, according to Luke, all the disciples ask, "Lord, shall we strike with a sword?" (Luke 22:49) Then one of the disciples "put his hand on his sword, drew it, and struck the high priest's servant, cutting off his ear." Matthew's, Mark's, and Luke's unnamed disciple attempts to defend Jesus by using the same means as the arresting authorities. John's Gospel, however, goes further by naming the sword-wielding disciple as none other than Peter himself. Shortly thereafter, this Peter, who is willing to kill to protect Jesus, will deny three times that he even knows Jesus. Perhaps Peter, like the disciples and the rest of us, resorts to violence because he is more interested in protecting himself than in protecting Jesus.

The disciples are unable to comprehend Jesus' way of nonviolence. Over and over, Jesus instructs them to love their enemies and to lay down their lives for one another, thus preparing them for confrontation with the ruling authorities and the inevitable outcome. But the disciples never understand Jesus. They hear his Sermon on the Mount, and they celebrate the Passover meal with him. But they keep asking, "Lord, shall we strike with a sword?"

I have to go easy on the disciples, though, because I know how slow I am in my own heart to accept Jesus' way of the cross. Today, priests, bishops, theologians, cardinals, popes, monks, religious, and Christians of every stripe still ask, "Lord, shall we strike with a sword?" When wars heat up, revolutions foment, and violence threatens, we call out, "Lord, shall we strike with a sword?"—and rarely does anyone wait for an answer. To our all-American minds, there can be only one answer: "Yes." The swords and guns and bombs come out, and people are stabbed, shot, napalmed, electrocuted, gassed, obliterated, decimated. We strike with a sword—and so much more. We cut off an ear—and so much more. We destroy entire countries and incinerate hundreds of thousands of people in a flash. In fact, we're willing to risk the destruction of the entire planet, if necessary, to defend ourselves. Again and again, we strike back with violence to protect ourselves. We carry on, thanks to the ever-present, ever-trusty, ever-faithful, sword.

At this climactic point in the story of Jesus, as the soldiers put their hands on him, arrest him, and take him away, Jesus turns to the disciples for the final time. As he is dragged away by the authorities, he tells his community once again to reject violence:

> "Put your sword back into its sheath, for all who take the sword will perish by the sword. Do you think that I cannot call upon my Father and he will not provide me at this moment with more than twelve legions of angels? But then how would the scriptures be fulfilled which say that it must come to pass in this way?" (Matthew 26:52–55)

Jesus invokes God and God's nonviolent armies (the thousands of angels) who would answer if called, but he keeps his eye on the Scriptures. He will not become a murderous, imperial messiah; he is the nonviolent Suffering Servant of Isaiah. He is a peacemaking, sacrificial God.

Put your sword back! These are the last words—a definitive rebuke—
the disciples hear from Jesus before they run away. If ever there was a
moment in God's eyes when violence would be justifiable, this is it! But
Jesus is clear: *Put your sword back!* His followers are not allowed to respond
with violence. They are not allowed to kill. They are not allowed to harm
others. They are not allowed to threaten others. They are not permitted to
"deter" violent crime with the use of violence.

Why? Because all those who take up the sword shall perish by the
sword. Violence begets violence. Killing begets killing. Nukes beget more
nukes. Death begets death. Jesus, the incarnation of the God of nonviolence, stands for life. He will not succumb to the way of violence. Although
he knows that he will perish under the cross's violence, he places his hope
in the God of Life and awaits that third day.

Put your sword back! The command stands as the ultimate reproof of
violence. From Christ's perspective—the perspective of one who is under
arrest and in trouble with the authorities—our violence reveals that we
have sided with the empire, that we are no different from the oppressive
authorities. But Jesus, wanting us to break free from the cycle of violence,
outlaws violent retaliation. Earlier, he surpasses Isaiah's vision of "beating
swords into plowshares" by calling his followers to love their enemies. Now,
when the authorities seize him, his command remains urgent but more
modest: "Put back your sword." He will not permit violence under any
circumstances. Luke's translation makes an equally all-encompassing, blan-
ket condemnation of violence: *"Stop, no more of this!"* (22:51)

Those of us who would follow Jesus are precluded from drawing the
sword. We are people who love our enemies; who prefer to undergo violence rather than inflict it upon others; who reject every form of violence,
from nuclear weapons to chemical weapons to Trident submarines to handguns. We oppose the Stealth Bomber, the B52, the F22, the MX, the cruise
missile, the latest nuclear technology, Livermore Laboratories, the S.A.C.
Base, the marines, the CIA, the FBI, the army, the navy, and all perpetra-
tors of violence and their arsenals. We renounce war and violent self-defense,
tear up the just-war theory, and embrace gospel nonviolence. We not only
put back any swords we have, but we beat them into plowshares. The unarmed Christ disarms us. Christ's community, the Church, is a community
of nonviolence.

Does this mean that Christians cannot be employed by the Pentagon, the police, or the nuclear-weapons manufacturers? The question goes to the heart of Jesus' message. If we will obey the last words of Jesus, then we will not, like Judas, side with the imperial authorities—and we will not employ their means of violence. We will refuse to carry weapons, even for the noblest reason, and we will not work for any institution that inflicts violence. We prepare, instead, to undergo what Christ undergoes.

Jesus issues this final command—and his disciples turn and run away. They run not only from the imperial authorities who threaten the entire discipleship community; they run from the unarmed, nonviolent Christ who will not defend himself against personal harm. They know that an unarmed response to the imperial authorities will lead to disappearance, torture, and execution—and who can stomach such craziness? The Evangelists do not cover up the rejection Jesus undergoes: *All the disciples left him and fled.* Jesus is left alone once again, for the last time. He is led away to be slaughtered.

"Have you come out as against a robber, with swords and clubs to seize me?" Jesus asks the authorities. "Day after day I sat teaching in the Temple area, yet you did not arrest me. But all this has come to pass that the writings of the prophets may be fulfilled." Jesus condemns the military and religious authorities. As Ched Myers observes, he scolds them for treating him as "a robber":

> It is significant that Jesus is taken as a representative of the rural resistance, just as he will be crucified as one ("between two robbers"). Jesus may reject armed resistance, but he understands it; his disdain is reserved for state violence, which forever passes its provocation off as "prevention." . . . Jesus taunts the authorities with the fact that their ambush only unmasks their political impotence: what they could not do in public they do covertly. Finally, Jesus throws back in the teeth of his opponents the higher and deeper authority: the "scriptures." Mark cites no specific text, as if he is alluding to the entire "script" of biblical radicalism. This script is now "fulfilled." . . . It is this script that the leaders cannot understand and that the disciples cannot follow. When the latter realize that he does not intend to turn away from his fidelity to this script, they flee for their lives.[1]

In the end, Jesus remains faithful to the Scriptures and to the God of the Scriptures. He maintains his nonviolence, loves his enemies, speaks the truth, condemns the empire, and trusts finally that the prophets have now been fulfilled. As he is led away, he has found meaning in his nonviolent resistance. He alone remains faithful to the God of nonviolence.

chapter twenty-eight

TRIAL

They led Jesus away to the high priest, and all the chief priests and the elders and the scribes came together. Peter followed him at a distance . . . The chief priests and the entire Sanhedrin kept trying to obtain testimony against Jesus in order to put him to death, but they found none. Many gave false witness against him, but their testimony did not agree. Some took the stand and testified falsely against him . . . [T]heir testimony did not agree. The high priest rose before the assembly and questioned Jesus, saying, "Have you no answer? What are these men testifying against you?" But he was silent and answered nothing. Again the high priest asked him and said to him, "Are you the Messiah, the son of the Blessed One?" Then Jesus answered, "I am;

> *and 'you will see the Son of Man
> seated at the right hand of the Power
> and coming with the clouds of heaven.'"*

At that the high priest tore his garments and said, "What further need have we of witnesses? You have heard the blasphemy. What do you think?" They all condemned him as deserving to die. Some began to spit on him. They blindfolded him and struck him and said to him, "Prophesy!" And the guards greeted him with blows. . . . As soon as morning came, the chief priests with the elders and the scribes, that is, the whole Sanhedrin, held a council. They bound Jesus, led him away, and handed him over to Pilate. Pilate questioned him, "Are you the king of the Jews?" He said to him in reply, "You say so." The chief priests accused him of many things. Again Pilate questioned him, "Have you no answer? See how many things they accuse you of." Jesus gave him no further answer. (Mark 14:53–57, 59–65; 15:1–5)

The hour has arrived. The religious authorities put Jesus on trial—secretly, in the dark of night. After an array of witnesses lie about Jesus, the authorities charge him with inciting revolt, opposing payment of taxes to Caesar, and claiming to be the Messiah (see Luke 23:1–5). Although the various accounts differ, Jesus endures rigged political trials and brutal interrogations before the Sanhedrin, the chief priests, Pilate, Herod, and a large crowd. He is convicted and sentenced to death. He never stood a chance.

In Mark's descriptions of the two political trials, one before the Sanhedrin and one before Pilate, false charges are raised, the authorities interrogate Jesus, and Jesus does not respond. Eventually, Jesus confesses—first that he is the Son of Humanity (Daniel's image of a nonviolent Being who rules the universe) and then that he is a king. The chief priests respond by torturing, beating, and mocking him. Although the Roman procurator, Pilate, defends Jesus' innocence and considers releasing him, the chief priests stir up the crowd—at which time, Pilate shows his true colors. He releases Barabbas, the convicted terrorist who "had been imprisoned for rebellion and murder" (Luke 23:25) and sentences Jesus to death.

According to Luke's version of the indictment, Jesus "is inciting the people with his teaching throughout all Judea, from Galilee where he began even to here" (23:5). Pilate sends him to Herod, who is glad to see Jesus, for he had:

> . . . been wanting to see him for a long time, for he had heard about him and had been hoping to see him perform some sign. He questioned him at length, but he gave him no answer. The chief priests and scribes, meanwhile, stood by accusing him harshly. (Even) Herod and his soldiers treated him contemptuously and mocked him, and after clothing him in resplendent garb, he sent him back to Pilate. Herod and Pilate became friends that very day, even though they had been enemies formerly (Luke 23:8–12).

The authorities are determined to do away with Jesus from the start.

John's Gospel explains that Jesus is bound and brought first to Annas, the father-in-law of Caiaphas the high priest, the one "who had counseled the Jews that it was better that one man should die rather than the people" (John 18:14). After Annas interrogates Jesus, Caiaphas and Pilate question him. Jesus responds more often in John's Gospel than in the other gospel accounts; he speaks of nonviolence, truth, power, and God:

> "My kingdom does not belong to this world. If my kingdom did belong to this world, my attendants (would) be fighting to keep me from being handed over to the Jews. But as it is, my kingdom is not here." So Pilate said to him, "Then you are a king?" Jesus answered, "You say I am a king. For this I was born and for this I came into the world, to testify to the truth. Everyone who belongs to the truth listens to my voice" (18:36–37).

Later, after being scourged, mocked, and tortured with thorns, Jesus is brought before Pilate for further interrogation, but he does not respond. "Do you not speak to me?" Pilate asks, "Do you not know that I have power to release you and I have power to crucify you?" (John 19:10) Finally, Jesus answers: "You would have no power over me if it had not been given to you from above. For this reason the one who handed me over to you has the greater sin" (John 19:11).

Jesus stands before representatives of the empire to speak of his own realm. He judges their conduct and announces that all who seek truth listen to his voice. In response, the authorities issue his death warrant because they see him as the empire's enemy. "If you release him, you are not a Friend of Caesar," the Judean authorities tell Pilate. "Everyone who makes himself a king opposes Caesar" (John 19:12). "Shall I crucify your king?" Pilate asks them. "We have no king but Caesar," the chief priests answer. So Pilate "handed him over to them to be crucified" (John 19:15–16).

In the Garden of Gethsemane, Jesus knows that once he is arrested he will be convicted quickly by the empire's judges who will defend the empire at all costs. He knows, too, that thousands already have died on the empire's crosses. Before such dominating power—and knowing himself to be defenseless—Jesus refuses to pledge allegiance to the empire, to Caesar, to Herod, to Pilate, to the Sanhedrin, or to death itself. Rather, he stands before the world's judges as one who pays no heed to the imperial laws of death, for he is not bound by death's rules. He lives by God's rule, by God's law, and in God's reign. His radiant truth, of course, threatens the established order. The authorities, understanding Jesus' permanent civil disobedience, snuff him out.

Throughout these judicial charades, Jesus remains nonviolent. Abused and tortured, he does not strike back or threaten anyone. He tells Annas:

> "I have spoken publicly to the world. I have always taught in a synagogue or in the temple area where all the Jews gather, and in secret I have said nothing. Why ask me? Ask those who heard me what I said to them. They know what I said" (John 18:20–21).

When one of the Temple guards strikes him, Jesus refuses to be humiliated. Instead, he clings to his dignity and responds humanly to the guard: "If I have spoken wrongly, testify to the wrong; but if I have spoke rightly, why do you strike me?" (John 18:23)

After responding several times to their charges, and enduring incessant interrogation and torture, Jesus falls silent. By refusing to speak, Jesus refuses to acknowledge the authority of the court, the empire, its laws, and its dehumanizing violence. In his silence, the humiliated Jesus speaks loudly against the courts of death. When the entire system bears down upon an innocent person, and every nonviolent alternative of resistance has run its course, silence becomes the final form of noncooperation.

When we stood trial in Elizabeth City, North Carolina, for our Plowshares demonstration, I could not have imagined the farcical trial the authorities would stage against us. They were determined to crush us and other antinuclear activists before a larger movement developed. As we entered the courtroom, the prosecutor and the judge issued a joint statement ordering us, under threat of contempt, not to mention the U.S. government, military, air force, or nuclear arsenal, or to make any reference to international law, Nuremberg principles, philosophy, theology, the Bible, or God. How does one respond to fascism under the guise of democracy?

We decided to speak out. In our opening statement, we denounced our government's nuclear and military arsenal, the court's defense of militarism, and our unjust, undemocratic treatment by the courts, and we called people to conversion to the God of peace. We were immediately cited with contempt charges and a mistrial was declared.

Months later, when four separate trials were held for each of us, we were prevented from offering any relevant information about our action, the motives behind it, or the urgent demands of disarmament. Three of us futilely offered a few arguments, but by the fourth trial, Lynn Fredriksson, our last group member, decided that the best way she could protest this unjust treatment was to sit silently throughout the proceedings. She made a brief opening statement explaining her noncooperation with the judicial charade, and then sat in silence while the prosecutor and the judge tried her. A jury found her guilty in less than fifteen minutes.

Her silent testimony spoke loud and clear.

With a few choice words, Jesus testifies to the truth. Earlier, he had urged his disciples to speak the truth when they are hauled before judges and governors (see Luke 12:10). In such circumstances, he says, the Spirit will give you the words to speak and the truth will set you free (see John 8:32). His silence is his final protest and, in his silence, Jesus repudiates the system, the empire, the courts, their laws, and the metaphors of death. He is free. Jesus reverses the roles between defendant and judge. In his silence, he becomes the judge—and everyone else stands trial.

The gospel proclaims this hour of judicial charade as the moment of glory. The Son of Humanity appears, and the imperial courts, their laws, and the world are found guilty. The truth of nonviolence condemns the world's violence.

chapter twenty-nine

THE WHOLE COHORT

Then the soldiers of the governor took Jesus inside the praetorium and gathered the whole cohort around him. They stripped off his clothes and threw a scarlet military cloak about him. Weaving a crown out of thorns, they placed it on his head, and a reed in his right hand. And kneeling before him, they mocked him, saying, "Hail, King of the Jews!" They spat upon him and took the reed and kept striking him on the head. And when they had mocked him, they stripped him of the cloak, dressed him in his own clothes, and led him off to crucify him. (Matthew 27:27–30)

Matthew's account of the sufferings of Jesus paints an awesome, terrible moment that occurs just after Jesus is condemned to death. The Roman soldiers lead Jesus inside the praetorium, the Jerusalem residence of the Roman governor, which is an enormous military fortress. There, Matthew tells us, they gather "the whole cohort" around him.

The whole cohort! According to biblical scholars, the whole cohort of Roman soldiers amounts to six hundred soldiers who are brought into Jerusalem to protect the Roman governor during the festival in the event of a riot or rebellion.

We remember the breathtaking image of the young Chinese student standing before the imperial tanks in Tiannamon Square in Beijing. But this scene of Jesus, surrounded by six hundred jeering, laughing, murderous Roman soldiers, stops the heart. It is one of the most appalling, astounding, amazing images presented in the Scriptures.

Jesus spends his days teaching and practicing nonviolence as the way of life; he is the fullness of nonviolence. In order to be faithful to his nonviolent God, he denounces all the violence of the world, most especially the oppressive violence of the empire. Yet, here he is, condemned to death and brought before six hundred soldiers. These poor people spend their days torturing and crucifying others in the name of the emperor. They do not believe in God or pretend to know anything about justice or compassion, so they bring the full brunt of the imperial army upon Jesus, humiliating him as no one has ever been humiliated.

First they strip him—and that's when the mocking begins. Then, when he is covered with blood from the many wounds of his scourging, they put a "scarlet military cloak" around him (which does not cover him). Then they weave a crown of thorns for his head and place a reed, like a royal scepter, in his hand. They mock him, spit on him, strike him in the head, interrogate him, laugh at him, beat him and, finally, strip him again. Jesus undergoes complete and total humiliation—in front of six hundred mean, ruthless, brutal soldiers.

I believe this scene by Matthew is the most antimilitary image ever written. God stands mocked, tortured, abused, naked, and laughed at by the entire Roman army in Jerusalem. In this moment, we see all the militaries and all the armies of the world mocking and laughing at Jesus. The soldiers hate Jesus, humiliate him, and torture him, because he claims to be a king, to be God. Since, in their eyes, there is no God—surely this naked, helpless man is not the eternal God—then he is the biggest fool they have ever encountered. The whole claim of Jesus is so preposterous to them as to be hilarious.

What they do not know, of course, is that this indeed is God, the God who created them, the God of the universe, the God of history, standing before them.

Every military army, by definition, hates God. The purpose of a military, after all, is to kill human beings. Because God dwells in every human being and outlaws killing, any army stands in direct opposition to God. The spirit within any and every army is anti-God, anti-life, anti-Christ. It is demonic.

If, as Christians, we are not convinced that God does not condone war, that God is not warlike, and that God does not support militarism, then we need to spend more time standing with the mocked Jesus as he suffers the jeers and humiliations of six hundred Roman soldiers just before they kill him. If we contemplate this scene and still desire to follow the rebel Jesus, then we will know that we cannot belong to any military in any nation at anytime under any circumstances. Indeed, we will never be able to be drafted; we will never be able to support a military; we will never be able to pay for a military; we will never be able to kill for a military. From now on, like the rebel Jesus, like God, we will be an antimilitary people. We will allow ourselves, in our nonviolence, truth, and resistance to militarism, to be humiliated and run over by the militaries of the world. With Christ, we will allow the world's armies to crush us rather than pay them allegiance or deny God's way of nonviolence.

If we are going to follow Jesus, we, too, will have to share in the humiliation of confronting the militaries of the world, denouncing their violence, and suffering their abuse. With the hidden God of nonviolence, we will confront the whole cohort and undergo derision and abuse. And in that hour, in that crucible, we will learn what faith in our beloved, nonviolent God means.

chapter thirty

THE LOUD CRY

They brought him to the place of Golgotha . . . They gave him wine drugged with myrrh, but he did not take it. Then they crucified him and divided his garments by casting lots for them to see what each should take. It was nine o'clock in the morning when they crucified him. The inscription of the charge against him read, "The King of the Jews." With him they crucified two revolutionaries, one on his right and one on his left. Those passing by reviled him, shaking their heads and saying, "Aha! You who would destroy the temple and rebuild it in three days, save yourself by coming down from the cross." Likewise the chief priests, with the scribes, mocked him among themselves and said, "He saved others; he cannot save himself. Let the Messiah, the King of Israel, come down now from the cross that we may see and believe." Those who were crucified with him also kept abusing him.

At noon darkness came over the whole land until three in the afternoon. And at three o'clock Jesus cried out in a loud voice, . . . "My God, my God, why have you forsaken me?" Some of the bystanders who heard it said, "Look, he is calling Elijah." One of them ran, soaked a sponge with wine, put it on a reed, and gave it to him to drink, saying, "Wait, let us see if Elijah comes to take him down." Jesus gave a loud cry and breathed his last. (Mark 15:22–37)

Jesus is stripped and crucified. As he hangs dying on the cross, the soldiers offer him wine, but he turns it down, choosing instead to face pain and death head on. Hanging on the cross for hours, Jesus experiences the depth of human pain; he is completely and utterly rejected. As he receives verbal abuse from passersby and those crucified with him, he calls out to God, gives one last outburst—"a loud cry"—and breathes his last.

Jesus dies as he lived: fully conscious, alert, and alive. But, nonetheless, he dies.

Jesus' only supporters, Mark records, are a handful of Galilean women, including Mary Magdalene and another Mary, who may be Jesus' mother, now described as a disciple (see Mark 15:40–41). The others—the passersby, the chief priests, and the revolutionaries—mock the dying Jesus, saying, "Save yourself by coming down from the cross!" They show no trace of compassion. Quite the contrary, in fact; they blast Jesus' faith in God.

After hanging on the cross in agony for hours, Jesus, too, protests. He calls out, "My God, my God, why have you forsaken me?" While biblical scholars have rightly pointed out the Evangelists' reference to Psalm 22, a hymn of hope and victory, it begins, nonetheless, as a cry of despair. Jesus feels abandoned by God.

What does this mean? If Jesus, the most faithful, truest person who ever lived, feels abandoned by God, why should the rest of us expect to feel otherwise? Who among us should hope to feel comforted and united with a loving God when Jesus himself felt so rejected at the hour of his death?

The scene stops us in our tracks. If we are honest, we understand the passersby, the chief priests, and the revolutionaries. We claim sympathy with Jesus, but we more often reject his trusting faith and steadfast nonviolence. In our despair, we, too, put him down. Who of us can accept the crucifixion of Jesus—and his acceptance of it?

As darkness covers the land, Jesus tastes rock-bottom despair; he knows his last breath is approaching. In his life of nonviolent resistance, he has done everything he could to awaken people to the realities of life and death. And because he tried to serve everyone every moment of his life, it stands to reason that he will use even the moment of his death as a gift to humanity. "What can I do?" he no doubt asks himself. "What last gift can I offer?"

Those who are crucified die by suffocation; they have no strength left to lift their lungs and breathe. According to Mark's account, Jesus uses his dying breath as one last act of protest. The Evangelist describes Jesus gathering every last ounce of strength to take one deep breath. Instead of dying silently, quietly, until his breathing is no longer evident, Jesus bursts out with "a loud cry." All the energy within him goes with that final outburst—and he dies.

That loud cry. When all is said and done, after all the sermons, blessings, and chastisements, Jesus cries out loudly. He makes one last appeal beyond silence and beyond words. He cries out to God and to every human heart. It is his last act.

The passersby, the chief priests, and the revolutionaries simply shake their heads. Luke records that when the crowd "who had gathered for this spectacle saw what had happened, they returned home beating their breasts" (Luke 23:48). "Alas, what a shame!" they say. "He had such promise! If only he could have saved himself! If he was the Messiah, he would have come down from that cross. If he was God, he would have done something. But he wasn't. He was a fool. So much for nonviolence. It is ineffective. Nothing can challenge the empire's death penalty or death itself." They keep on walking—and they let him die.

Even those dying next to Jesus verbally abuse him. Mark records no beautiful declaration of faith: "Jesus, remember me, when you come into your kingdom."

Jesus dies a complete failure. No one believes in him. In the end, even God abandons him—or so it seems.

The Gospels insist that God chose to become fully human in Jesus. But instead of clinging to divinity, Christ humbles himself to taste the fullness of humanity. By becoming fully human, he becomes fully nonviolent. He is born in poverty, lives poorly, loves humanly, resists evil, and suffers in absolute poverty unto death on the cross. In keeping with his mission, he does not resort to violence. Rather, he challenges the empire and its injustice, and suffers its death penalty. His loud cry is a protest of death, a protest of crucifixion, a protest of the cold-blooded passersby who show no sign of compassion.

I wonder if I have ever heard it—this loud cry. I have only recently noticed it in this story.

In Jesus' loud cry, I hear the cry of the poor and the oppressed throughout human history. In his cry, I hear the cry of all victims of injustice, war, and empire. I hear the dead of Hiroshima and Nagasaki, Auschwitz and Dresden, My Lai and Baghdad, Rwanda and Sarajevo, El Mozote and San Quentin, East Timor and Tibet, Sudan and Northern Ireland, South Central Los Angeles and Camden, New Jersey. In his loud cry, I hear God begging humanity to wake up to reality, to reject the insanity of violence, to repent of its inhumanity, and to turn a compassionate heart toward those who suffer. And who hears that loud cry?

To hear the loud cry of Jesus is to let our hearts be broken. If we hear that loud cry echoing today in the dying, in those crushed by the state, we will be moved to reach out with compassion. If we hear the cry of resisters and oppressed peoples, we will want to protest and prevent their suffering and executions.

One thinks of Franz Jagerstatter, beheaded by the Nazis for refusing to kill for them. And of Steve Biko, tortured in a South African prison cell, then driven through the night in the back of a police van, his wounded head bouncing on the metal floor until he dies. And of Rutilio Grande, El Salvador's Jesuit priest who called for justice and who was assassinated in 1977 by U.S.-backed government death squads while driving his jeep from one village Mass to another. And of the six Jesuit priests of the Jesuit university in San Salvador, dragged outside at two o'clock in the morning, forced to lie on the ground, shot in the head, and their brains removed. And of Elba Ramos, their cook, and Celina, her sixteen-year-old daughter, machine-gunned on a couch in a parlor where, in terror, they had tried to hide while the Jesuits were murdered outside. And of the countless anonymous Christians of the first three centuries who were crucified, beheaded, or fed to the lions for refusing to kill for the empire—killed for worshiping the nonviolent Christ. The litany goes on.

If we let that loud cry touch our hearts, we, too, will give our lives as Jesus did. We, too, will risk our lives on the way of the nonviolence. We, too, will disobey the imperial laws of injustice and risk martyrdom. We, too, will join ourselves to his loud cry. Along the way, we, too, will understand the truth that not only did he save himself but his loving, faithful endurance saved all humanity. He becomes "our ransom from death," as the early church testified.

The Loud Cry continues.

From now on, we are people of the Loud Cry, people of nonviolence, resisters of death. Our message: The killing must end. The violence stops here, in his body, in our bodies—now.

chapter thirty-one

RISEN

On the evening of that first day of the week, when the doors were locked, where the disciples were, for fear of the Jews, Jesus came and stood in their midst and said to them, "Peace be with you." When he had said this, he showed them his hands and his side. The disciples rejoiced when they saw the Lord. (Jesus) said to them again, "Peace be with you. As the Father has sent me, so I send you." And when he had said this, he breathed on them and said to them, "Receive the holy Spirit. Whose sins you forgive are forgiven them, and whose sins you retain are retained." (John 20:19–23)

On the first day of the week, Mary Magdalene and the other women rise early and walk to the tomb to anoint the body of Jesus. According to the various gospel accounts, the women see that the stone has been rolled away and that the tomb is empty. Then, when an angel greets them, the women are "terrified," "filled with fear," "amazed," and "bow their heads to the ground." In Luke, the angel asks:

"Why do you seek the living one among the dead? He is not here, but he has been raised. Remember what he said to you while he was still in Galilee, that the Son of Man must be handed over to sinners and be crucified, and rise on the third day" (24:5–7).

According to Mark, the angel says:

"Go and tell his disciples and Peter, 'He is going before you to Galilee; there you will see him, as he told you.'" Then they went out and fled from the tomb, seized with trembling and bewilderment. They said nothing to anyone, for they were afraid (16:7–8).

I am amazed that Jesus would be willing to return. He has been betrayed, denied, abandoned, and executed; all his friends left him alone to die. How would we feel about such friends after such rejection? We would be angry, hurt, resentful; we would probably have nothing to do with our friends ever again. Yet, here comes Jesus, forgiving us, calling us to be his community, intimately inviting us to touch his wounds and giving us God's own peace. Jesus keeps coming back, forever making peace with humanity.

All the resurrection accounts begin with fear. When the risen Jesus first appears to his friends, they are in hiding behind locked doors because they are afraid. To enter the resurrection story, we need to run from the tomb with the terrified women, sit with the disciples in their fear, and face our own fears—fear of change, fear of loss, fear of rejection, fear of insecurity, fear of being alone, fear of the unknown, fear of the future, fear of God, fear of arrest, fear of suffering, and fear of death. The risen Jesus walks into this climate of fear and says, "Peace be with you"—and their fear turns to joy. Their community of fear is transformed into a community of joy.

Each Gospel presents the Resurrection of Jesus in different ways. Mark's version, the earliest of the narratives, abruptly ends with the angel calling the disciples to return to Galilee and the women fleeing in fear from the empty tomb. (Mark 16:9–20, by all accounts, was added centuries later, probably to make the Gospel more manageable.) As Ched Myers writes, Mark leaves the story unfinished, in our hands. If we want to know what happens, we, like the disciples, must also return to Galilee and take up the story ourselves. It is our turn to enter the narrative, to walk, like Jesus, from our own, modern-day, poverty-stricken Galilee to face the imperial authorities and institutionalized injustice in Jerusalem, on the way of nonviolence to the cross. Along that way, we will meet the risen Jesus and understand the story. Then we will worship him as our Lord and Savior.

Matthew's account describes a great earthquake and the descent of an angel from heaven who approaches the tomb, rolls back the stone, and sits upon it. "His appearance was like lightning and his clothing was white as snow" (Matthew 28:3), and the Roman guards are "shaken with fear and became like dead men" (Matthew 28:4). The angel then says:

"Do not be afraid! I know that you are seeking Jesus the crucified. He is not here, for he has been raised just as he said. Come and see the place where he lay. Then go quickly and tell his disciples, 'He has been raised from the dead, and he is going before you to Galilee; there you will see him.' Behold, I have told you" (28:5–7).

As the women run away "fearful yet overjoyed," they meet Jesus, fall at his feet, and worship him. "Do not be afraid," he tells them. "Go tell my brothers to go to Galilee, and there they will see me" (Matthew 28:8–10). Matthew, too, enjoins us to take up the story where Jesus left off, to start it again.

In John's Gospel, as Mary Magdalene stands weeping outside the empty tomb, a gardener asks her why she is crying. "Whom are you looking for?" Jesus asks. Then, when he calls her by name, she recognizes him, falls at his feet, and does him homage. But he says to her, "Stop holding on to me, for I have not yet ascended to the Father. But go to my brothers and tell them, 'I am going to my Father and your Father, to my God and your God.'" Mary Magdalene obeys. She goes to the disciples and declares, "I have seen the Lord" (John 20:15, 17–18)—but they do not believe her.

Later that day, Jesus appears to the disciples in their hideout. He greets them with words of peace, shows them the wounds in his hands and side, and repeats his greeting a second time: "Peace be with you!" John's Jesus deliberately connects resurrection with peace, a peace that does not deny Jesus' agony and death. Rather, the peace of the risen Lord comes through the wounds of the cross. The risen One gives us peace as we accept his wounds, his cross—as we share his way of nonviolent resistance to evil, even to the point of undergoing persecution, arrest, suffering, and death.

In other words, if we want to be people of resurrection, if we want to receive Christ's peace, we must recognize, understand, and embrace his wounds, his cross. It all goes together. John's Gospel concludes with an invitation to accept the wisdom of the paschal mystery.

Every Good Friday, thousands of Christians walk along 42nd Street in New York City, from the United Nations to Times Square, on the annual Pax Christi "Stations of the Cross." We remember the traditional sufferings of Christ and the ongoing sufferings of Christ in the current wars and injustices of the world—and their connections in downtown New York, from Time Squares' Armed Forces Recruiting Station to Grand Central Station's police sweeps against the homeless. In 1997, thirty-two of us celebrated the fifteenth station, the Resurrection, by holding up banners calling for peace and disarmament in the plaza at the Intrepid War Museum, a destroyer that has been turned into a museum for the purpose of glorifying war. We were arrested, held for a few hours, and released. We were trying to walk Jesus' way of the cross, to break out of our fear, to speak the truth of Christ's peace, to spread his message of nonviolence, and to receive his peace.

A few weeks before our civil disobedience, the senior class at Fordham University, where I was teaching theology, announced that its senior ball would be held on board the Intrepid War Museum. Some of us spoke out against the dance, explaining that the Intrepid War Museum, like the Pentagon and every military base in the country, stands as an affront to the risen Lord and his gift of peace. Such a scene reenacts the biblical story of the exiled, frustrated, faithless Hebrews dancing around the golden calf, mocking God.

The Fordham senior class's decision and the largely silent support of the faculty, administration, and Jesuit community offer a strong symbol for our times. As a propaganda arm of the Pentagon, the Intrepid Museum proudly displays nuclear missiles, attack and bomber jets, and a destroyer that shelled Vietnamese villages during the Vietnam War. It also exhibits U.S. weapons that were used to bomb hundreds of thousands of people during the Gulf War massacre. The museum includes an A-4 Skyhawk, a fighter jet used by the Kuwaiti military to kill people during the Gulf War; a Tomahawk cruise missile, capable of carrying nuclear weapons; and the *U.S.S. Growler* submarine, one of the first ships to carry nuclear weapons. An army M-42 antiaircraft artillery vehicle and M-60 Patton tank are parked in the plaza. This ship-turned-museum, the *U.S.S. Intrepid,* dropped thousands of tons of bombs on the people of Vietnam and Laos.

Throughout its existence, the Intrepid War Museum has received millions of dollars in government subsidies, including hundreds of thousands of dollars from the financially strapped Board of Education. It also received four and a half million dollars from the U.S. Department of Housing and Urban Development—funds that should have been used to provide low-income housing for the poor—to renovate the pier where it is berthed.

Most Jesuits, faculty, and students saw no problem with a party at the pro-war museum. As one Jesuit theologian at Fordham told me, "We're all Niebuhrians here. Coercion and war are necessary and justifiable. Jesus' ethic can't be applied socially; he never meant it to be. So what's wrong with a party on the *Intrepid?*" One Fordham senior wrote in the school newspaper: "My most stressful moral investigation concerning the ball is deciding on a dress. Does this make me shallow? No, just able to have a good time."

With ROTC training students on campus to carry weapons and kill, it is easy to see why few students or faculty members would not oppose the senior ball on the *Intrepid.* In such an environment, the Jesuit vision of the "faith that does justice" and the gospel command to "love your enemies" are easily dismissed as irrelevant ideals.

A few lone voices, however, kept raising questions. "I hope that future senior committees realize that many students at Fordham have problems with death, torture, and destruction in the name of military action," one senior wrote in the student paper. Philosophy professor Jim Marsh commented:

> I am deeply offended—intellectually, aesthetically, morally, politically, and religiously—by the senior class's decision to hold its senior ball on the *Intrepid,* ship of death, symbol of empire, and celebration of all that is most evil in the U.S. military industrial complex.

In the end, the seniors' selection showed not just bad taste or moral blindness, but the university's failure to educate its students in the Jesuit/Christian vision. It symbolizes how far we have come from the risen Christ's gift of peace.

The gospel teaches that if we are people of resurrection, we are also people of peace. From now on, we reject violence, war, weapons, bombs, nuclear weapons, ROTC, the military, injustice, the *Intrepid,* the Pentagon, and death. We have put down the swords, even beaten them into plowshares. We have been disarmed and called to the risen life of nonviolence.

The risen Lord deliberately shows us the wounds he received for his peacemaking efforts. He greets us with his invitation to peace and then sends us out, as he was sent, with that message of peace. He breathes upon us that we might live in his holy spirit of peace, that our breathing may be mindful, calm, and peaceful. From now on, we prefer to undergo the cross and to share his wounds, rather than inflict the cross on anyone else, including our enemies. We will never wound another person again.

The risen Jesus, according to John's account, leaves us two specific peacemaking tasks. First, we are to forgive one another. If we live in a spirit of resurrection peace, we cannot hold resentments or grudges, much less enact violence, vengeance, or war. We willingly forgive one another as Jesus forgives us. Second, we build communities of peace with one another. The original Greek is usually mistranslated. It should not read: "Whose sins you forgive are forgiven them; and whose sins you retain are retained." Rather, a better translation would be: "Those people you forgive are forgiven and those people you retain together in community are retained together as a community." In other words, forgive one another and stay together as a community.

John's Gospel enlarges the story further. Because Thomas is not present when Jesus appears, he refuses to believe that Jesus has risen unless he sees for himself the Lord's wounds. A week later, when the community sits together in fear behind locked doors—and this time Thomas is present—Jesus appears again. "Peace be with you," he says. The locked doors signify, among other things, that Jesus' disciples still are not at peace. They have not accepted his peace because they are still afraid. Perhaps they are afraid because they still do not believe in him.

Yet, here he comes again, hoping they will receive his peace, hoping they will put their faith in him. "Put your finger here," he says to Thomas, "and see my hands, and bring your hand and put it into my side, and do not be unbelieving, but believe." Those imperative verbs! Thomas obeys and a breakthrough occurs. "My Lord and my God!" (John 20:27–28)

This Gospel was probably written during the reign of Emperor Diocletian, who ordered that he was to be addressed as "My Lord and my God." If anyone worshiped some god other than the emperor with this title, he or she was to be immediately arrested and executed. Thomas and John's community break the imperial law by calling Jesus "My Lord and my God." Their proclamation announces not only their faith, but their willingness to die as martyrs. Those who hear this Gospel proclaimed, and accept its testimony, will likewise risk martyrdom.

But Jesus remains skeptical. "Have you come to believe because you have seen me?" After everything we have heard, the question lingers deliberately in the present tense. "Do you really believe in me?" The risen Lord questions their—and our—sincerity of faith.

Do we really believe in Jesus? The Gospel invites us to believe, to take another look at our fears, to welcome the risen Lord into our hearts, to accept his gift of peace, to touch his wounds, to forgive those who hurt us, and to build community with one another. More, it challenges us to carry on his witness of nonviolent resistance against the imperial forces of death, the demons of war, from Rome to America. If we respond like Thomas and confess Jesus our Lord and our God, we will receive the Lord's final gift, the gospel's last beatitude: We will be blessed.

Jesus' resurrection summons us to a life of peace, reconciliation, and faith. It confronts our fear of death and fills us with Christ's own joy. It calls us to topple the idols of death, to renounce our weapons, to outlaw war, and to pledge nonviolence. As we receive the peace of the risen Christ, we are disarmed, ready to welcome heaven's merciful peace here on earth. For the rest of our lives, we walk in the faith that comes from resurrection, the faith that makes peace. We reconcile with one another, build community with one another, and enjoy our life together in Christ's peace. We go forward saying "no" to death in all its legal, patriotic, military might.

We are more than blessed. We are saved.

chapter thirty-two

COME, HAVE BREAKFAST

When it was already dawn, Jesus was standing on the shore; but the disciples did not realize that it was Jesus. Jesus said to them, "Children, have you caught anything to eat?" They answered him, "No." So he said to them, "Cast the net over the right side of the boat and you will find something." So they cast it, and were not able to pull it in because of the number of fish. So the disciple whom Jesus loved said to Peter, "It is the Lord." When Simon Peter heard that it was the Lord, he tucked in his garment, for he was lightly clad, and jumped into the sea. The other disciples came in the boat, for they were not far from shore, only about a hundred yards, dragging the net with the fish. When they climbed out on shore, they saw a charcoal fire with fish on it and bread. Jesus said to them, "Bring some of the fish you just caught." So Simon Peter went over and dragged the net ashore full of one hundred fifty-three large fish. Even though there were so many, the net was not torn. Jesus said to them, "Come, have breakfast.". . . When they had finished breakfast, Jesus said to Simon Peter, "Simon, son of John, do you love me more than these?" He said him, "Yes, Lord, you know that I love you." He said to him, "Feed my lambs." He then said to him a second time, "Simon, son of John, do you love me?" He said to him, "Yes, Lord, you know that I love you." He said to him, "Tend my sheep." He said to him the third time, "Simon, son of John, do you love me?" Peter was distressed that he said to him a third time, "Do you love me?" and he said to him, "Lord, you know everything; you know that I love you."(Jesus) said to him, "Feed my sheep. Amen, amen, I say to you, when you were younger, you used to dress yourself and go where you wanted; but when you grow old, you will stretch out your hands, and someone else will dress you and lead you where you do not want to go." He said this signifying by what kind of death he would glorify God. And when he had said this, he said to him, "Follow me." (John 21:4–12, 15–19)

The modesty of resurrection. The Gospel portrays the recently deceased, now risen Jesus with understatement, humility, and glowing humanity. The dark night is over. A new day dawns.

Jesus stands alone on the shore, calls out to his fishing friends, and tells them where to throw their nets—and they catch a tremendous amount of fish. Then they recognize him and hasten ashore speechless, astounded. "Come, have breakfast," he says. Amazed, overjoyed, his friends eat until they are full. As usual, he serves them.

Only days before, Simon Peter had denied three times knowing Jesus. While Jesus was being tortured, he stood warming his hands on the charcoal fire in the Roman imperial courtyard. Yet, he now sits with the others around another charcoal fire enjoying not the Last Supper but the First Breakfast. The setting is intimate and warm, and the disciples are surprised to see the risen Lord. They simply cannot imagine him rising from the dead and making them breakfast. We can hardly imagine it either. If we had been through the ordeal he had been through, if we had been tortured, executed, and resurrected, would our first task be to make breakfast for our friends, for the one's who had abandoned us?

Much is left unsaid—yet, the breakfast says it all. Jesus does not condemn Simon Peter or the others; he does not harbor resentment like the rest of us would. Neither does he pretend that nothing has happened. Rather, he seeks reconciliation, healing, and commitment. He pointedly asks Simon Peter, "Do you love me?"—not just once but three times.

We so often hear that God loves us, but there comes a point when God wants to know if we love God. Jesus wants to know, "Do you love me? Do you truly love me?"

Jesus gives Peter the chance to redeem himself by offering him an opportunity to reassert his love. By asking the question, Jesus reveals his own pain and need for intimate love. He vulnerably opens his heart and invites Peter to profess *agape,* unconditional love. Peter, however, pledges only *philia,* the limited love shared by relatives and friends. Peter's response is limited but nonetheless he answers "yes" to Jesus and, after each response, Jesus missions him. "Feed my lambs. Tend my sheep. Feed my sheep."

If we profess our love for Jesus, we will be asked to walk the way of the cross. At this point, for the first time in John's Gospel, Jesus explains the cross to Peter. "You will be taken where you do not want to go." You, too, will be arrested, jailed, tried, tortured, and killed. And for the first time in John's Gospel, Jesus invites Peter to the journey of discipleship. "Follow me," he says.

The risen Jesus shares his intimate, unconditional love with his friends, draws out their love for him, and summons them on the way of discipleship to the cross. The scene is at once touching and terrifying. We are touched by Jesus' service and love for his friends, for us. At the same time, we are terrified that this risen martyr now missions us to care for the poor and the oppressed and to give our lives, as he did, in nonviolent resistance to systemic injustice.

None of us wants to suffer and die as Jesus did, but the gospel explains that if we truly love Jesus as our Master and Lord, we will do whatever he asks, live as he lived and, if necessary, die as he died. If we can respond with Simon Peter that we love Jesus, we will find the strength to "follow" and to "go where we do not want to go."

In 1985, I heard the renowned spiritual writer Henri Nouwen speak at "Peace Pentecost," a church gathering at Catholic University in Washington, D.C. Nouwen preached for over an hour and a half, holding spellbound his audience of over one thousand people. Several times throughout his address, he interrupted himself to lead us in Taize chants.

Among other passages, Nouwen reflected on Jesus' question to Peter: "Do you love me?" That question, he declared, is the most important one of our lives, especially for those of us concerned about justice and peace. If you love Jesus, "You will stretch out your hands, and someone else will put a belt around you and lead you where you would rather not go," he said, quoting Jesus. Keep your eyes on Jesus, he insisted. Keep working for justice and peace, but do it with heartfelt devotion to the risen Lord. You will be led where you would rather not go, and you will be taken by the culture of death—but you will trust Jesus, you will want to be at his side, and you will find your life used by him to glorify the God of peace.

The day after Henri's powerful Pentecost sermon, I flew to El Salvador, where I met the university Jesuits who were later assassinated, worked for two months in a church-run refugee camp in a war zone, and traveled through Nicaragua's contra-war and Guatemala's military repression. Throughout those intense months, Jesus' question reverberated in my spirit: "Do you love me? Feed my lambs. Do you love me? Tend my sheep. Do you truly love me? Feed my sheep. Someone will put a belt around you and lead you where you would rather not go. Follow me."

As my assignment at the Calle Real refugee camp came to an end, our friends threw a going-away party for me and another Jesuit. One of the Salvadoran *campesinos* presented me with a gift, a belt that he and his family had proudly made. When the father, a thin, elderly *campesino* with weathered lines on his face and tattered clothes, offered it to me, Jesus' question—and Nouwen's urgency—took on new meaning for me: The poor of Central America were putting a belt around me and taking me where I would rather not go—into the life of resistance to U.S. war-making and its consequences. I felt missioned by Christ in the Central American poor to call the North American Church to repentance, conversion, an end to war-making and a commitment to nonviolence.

At a certain point, shortly before his assassination, Martin Luther King, Jr., observed that the commitment to justice and peace takes over one's life. You speak out; you put your body on the line; you resist the forces of death; and before you know it, you can no longer turn back. At that point Jesus asks us if we truly love him. He wants to know if we will be faithful to him as he was faithful to God, right into the crucible of death. Then he calls us to follow him where he went, to that place where we would rather not go. We go forward, trusting in Jesus, keeping our eyes on him, faithful to the way of nonviolence come what may. We go forward into the fearful unknown, into the dark night of resistance, because we have seen our risen Lord stand on the shore. We have shared that intimate breakfast, seen his wounds, and heard him ask us if we love him. We go forward filled with hope because a new day dawns, the sunrise of peace, the day of resurrection. We can follow Jesus with heartfelt love because we know he has loved us first, laid down his life for us, and asked us to do the same for him and one another.

Who can resist his intimate love, his human friendship, his risen life? We finish breakfast and set off on the journey of justice and peace.

chapter thirty-three

THE ROAD TO EMMAUS

*Two of them were going to a village seven miles from Jerusalem called
Emmaus, and they were conversing about all the things that had oc-
curred. And it happened that while they were conversing and debating,
Jesus himself drew near and walked with them, but their eyes were prevented from recognizing him. He asked them, "What are you discussing
as you walk along?" They stopped, looking downcast. One of them, named
Cleopas, said to him in reply, "Are you the only visitor to Jerusalem who
does not know of the things that have taken place there in these days?"
And he replied to them, "What sort of things?" They said to him, "The
things that happened to Jesus the Nazarene, who was a prophet mighty in
deed and word before God and all the people, how our chief priests and
rulers both handed him over to a sentence of death and crucified him.
But we were hoping that he would be the one to redeem Israel; and besides all this, it is now the third day since this took place. Some women
from our group, however, have astounded us: they were at the tomb early
in the morning and did not find his body; they came back and reported
that they had indeed seen a vision of angels who announced that he was
alive. Then some of those with us went to the tomb and found things just
as the women had described, but him they did not see." And he said to
them, "Oh, how foolish you are! How slow of heart to believe all that the
prophets spoke! Was it not necessary that the Messiah should suffer these
things and enter into his glory?" Then beginning with Moses and all the
prophets, he interpreted to them what referred to him in all the scriptures. As they approached the village to which they were going, he gave
the impression that he was going on farther. But they urged him, "Stay
with us, for it is nearly evening and the day is almost over." So he went in
to stay with them. And it happened that, while he was with them at
table, he took bread, said the blessing, broke it, and gave it to them. With
that their eyes were opened and they recognized him, but he vanished
from their sight. (Luke 24:13–31)*

There comes a time in the struggle for peace and justice when we hit rock bottom, when we want to give up, when the pain around us is too much to bear, when all hope seems lost. In that moment, our expectations of Jesus crash and we throw up our hands, fold up our tents, and admit defeat. We leave our community, our commitment, and our convictions, and turn our backs on Jesus and his mission—and head home.

On that day, on that long walk home, Jesus sneaks up on us, like Flannery O'Connor's ragged figure "flitting from tree to tree." "What are you discussing as you walk along?" he asks on our journey of despair— and, of course, we do not recognize him. We see only a stranger. We are downcast. We have no hope. We cannot look up. We do not look into his eyes.

"You must be the only one who does not know the things that have been going on lately," we tell our politically out-of-touch, traveling companion.

"What things?" he asks.

What things? After all he has been through, after his betrayal, arrest, torture, execution, and resurrection, Jesus asks, "What things?" The Gospel is a study in understatement. Instead of reprimanding us, yelling at us, or condemning us for killing him, the humble, risen Jesus listens to our complaints before speaking. He wants to know why we stray from the discipleship journey.

The two wayfarers speak of dashed hopes, of the state's execution of Christ, of the mysterious tale of resurrection, and of the plain fact that they do not see him anymore. "We had hoped . . . ," they lament, shaking their heads, limping along the road to Emmaus. "We had hoped. . . ."

That famous past pluperfect: *We had hoped!* How often we give up hope and give in to despair.

Hope keeps faith when all appears lost. Hope hangs in there when everyone else says, "Let's go." Hope is tested not in good times but in the crucible.

The two disciples have given up hope in Christ. We know well their despair. We, too, complain about our dashed hopes, the hope we had that things would change. We had hoped God would intervene. We had hoped humanity would stop its wars. We had hoped that the world would feed its poor and live in peace. We had hoped justice would come. We had hoped the Church would reform. We had hoped Jesus would be victorious. We had hoped death would not get the last word. We had hoped God's realm would come to earth. We had hoped. . . ." Alas for such hopes!

"God, you must be the only one who does not know what's going on," we mutter under our breath as we walk away from the Church, from the struggle for social change, from one another. "Don't you know about the government's crucifixion of the world's poor, its latest war, its latest nuclear submarine launch, its latest military spending increase? Don't you know nonviolence doesn't work against the culture of death?" we cry out. "We had hoped that Jesus would bring his reign here and now and take over Jerusalem in the name of Israel. But now we know: It will not happen. He was a utopian dreamer. His words are idealistic. They cannot be applied to today's global horrors. We have to get on with our lives. We have to survive in the real world. There's no point in wasting our time struggling for disarmament or justice with Jesus. We were wrong. He failed. He made no real difference—and we can't make a difference either. There's nothing that can be done. We have to go our own way now."

"How foolish you are!" the stranger tells us. "How slow of heart to believe all that the prophets spoke! Was it not necessary that the Messiah should suffer these things and enter into his glory?"

Was it not necessary?

The voice of despair cannot grasp such hope. No, it was not necessary for Jesus to be arrested, jailed, tortured, and executed. What difference did it make? The world is brimming with injustice, starvation, war, murder, and weapons of mass destruction. Things are worse now than during Jesus' earthly lifetime. We stand on the brink of environmental destruction, if not global warfare, with our weapons stockpile. Jesus' nonviolence has not been accepted, and the idols of greed and violence rule the world. His death gave birth to a Church, yes, but look at its sinfulness, its cooperation with oppression, its silence before global injustice, its unwillingness to risk nonviolent action, its sexism and racism and blindness. No, it was not necessary that Jesus suffer and die.

We want change here and now, immediately, on our terms. We want to see the results of a new world and we want to be part of that powerful takeover.

Jesus, however, sees things from a different perspective. Through the long-haul lens of history, he looks at every human being, from the beginning of time until the end of time. Looking at us with the eyes of God, he sees far beyond our limited, historical struggles. He knows the big picture.

And so Jesus will not, cannot, accept our despair. He is the voice of hope.

One can only marvel at Jesus' patience, insistence, shining vision. He has been crucified and raised from the dead, yet he goes back to square one. He engages the hopeless in discussion, explaining the entire story of salvation. He outlines the Scriptures to his friends, reviews the journey of faith from Moses through the prophets to himself, and explains the biblical path of nonviolent resistance that led him to the cross, new life, and glory. He invites them to see the wisdom of the paschal mystery and, in the process, without their knowing it, he opens their eyes, restores their vision, and renews their hope.

The Christ has not failed his mission, he explains. In fact, just the opposite is true. Christ has been raised. Indeed, the way of nonviolence has triumphed. God is glorified. The culture of death and destruction is crumbling. The old world is falling away and the new realm of God's peace and justice is at hand. Suffering, accepted in love in the pursuit of truth and justice, bears immeasurable fruit if one only believes and holds out for the long haul. Unearned suffering is redemptive. Christ has shown this. He has walked through the crucible of nonviolence and lives on. Not only has Christ's life born fruit, but it will continue to bear fruit throughout salvation history. God's reign of nonviolence and love has come in our midst, and the world will be transformed. The powers of death have been overcome, and peace is at hand. Indeed, every human being will be invited into the reign of God. The nonviolent Christ, crushed and now risen, will "draw all unto himself."

"Cheer up," Jesus tells them. "The struggle for peace and justice may be just beginning, but it has already been won!"

Talk about hope! They are astonished. Who can resist such glowing faith, such eye-opening vision, such contagious hope? This stranger believes that Christ's mission of justice and peace must be carried on even if there are no apparent results, because he is convinced that Christ has overcome the world and disarmed it.

They urge him to stay longer. They show kindness to him and offer him hospitality. "Come and eat with us," they tell Christ in disguise.

And he joins them at their table. He takes the bread, blesses it, breaks it, and gives it to them—and all at once they recognize him.

"Jesus! You're alive!"

Just then, he vanishes. Their hearts ablaze with hope, these disciples turn around and run back to the community. They have seen and now they believe.

The risen Jesus walks with us, encouraging us not to give up hope. But, as Luke's tale explains, he is not seen in the profession of the creed. He is not seen in the retelling of his life story. He is not seen in despair or faithlessness. He is recognized only when we offer hospitality to the stranger in our midst, when meals are shared, when the bread of hope is broken.

The disciples run back to Jerusalem, to the scene of the crime, to the community of nonviolent resistance. There, in that circle, they meet Jesus again. There, in the community of nonviolence, he gives them his final word: Peace!

In this time of moral confusion and spiritual blindness, who understands the things that happen around us? We do not see Christ in our midst. We feel overwhelmed by the government's militarism, oppression of the poor, protection of multinational corporations, indifference to the world's starving masses, weapons sales to tyrants, funding for dictators, ongoing environmental destruction, and spending cuts for education, healthcare, employment, and housing. We want the coming of a new world but we give up hope that change is possible. We fall into the culture's despair, believing that nothing can be done, that nonviolence does not make a difference, that the struggle for disarmament and justice is not worth the sacrifice.

But the risen Christ returns to us, urging us not to give up hope. He helps us remember the story of salvation and the history of nonviolent social change—right up through the abolitionist, civil rights, and antiwar movements. He invokes the wisdom of the cross and invites us to follow him into the glory of resurrection. As we hear the good news of hope, welcome the visionary stranger to our table, and break bread together, our hearts burn with excitement and we recognize Christ in our midst. Then, we return to the community of nonviolent resistance and carry on his campaign for peace. Filled with hope and the desire to be faithful to our risen Lord, we take up the life struggle where Jesus left off.

The risen Jesus is met on the road to Emmaus, the road of despair. As we confess our infidelity and despair to him, allow his faith and hope to rekindle the fire in our hearts, and recognize him in the breaking of the bread, we turn around—and the road to Emmaus becomes the road to Jerusalem. The road of despair becomes the road of hope. The road of death becomes the road of life.

Christ goes ahead of us while our hearts burn within us. All we need do is follow him on the road to peace.

CONCLUSION

The gospel of Jesus calls us to love in a time of indifference, hope in a time of despair, nonviolence in a time of violence, justice in a time of injustice, and life in a time of death. Jesus teaches us not only how to live but how to die; how to transform not only the world but our own broken hearts as well; not only how to believe but in whom to believe.

In the end, Jesus the rebel shows us the face of God. His revolution transcends all our hopes for a better world for, in Jesus, the reign of God is at hand, here and now, at this very moment in human history. All people are created and destined for that reign of love and mercy, where our beloved God dwells.

In Jesus, we meet our beloved God. From now on we know that our God is not a god of despair but the God of hope; not a god of wrath but the God of mercy; not a god of condemnation but the God of compassion; not a god of imperial power but the God of the cross; not a god of domination but the God of loving service; not a god of oppression but the God of liberation; not a god who blesses injustice but the God of justice; not a god of war but the God of peace; not a god of violence but the God of nonviolence; not a god of death but the God of Life. From now on we know that we have been created to share in the fullness of life, in God's own life of love and unending mercy.

God's revolution is greater than our most utopian dreams. And in Jesus, everything we could hope has come true—and much more besides. We can go forward into the future, following the rebel Jesus, seeking justice, making peace, practicing nonviolence, resisting the forces of war, and loving our enemies come what may, because from now on, we know who our God is and we will never be content until we enter God's reign and stand before our beloved God. We know where we are going, and we know the promise will be fulfilled. We have met Jesus the rebel. He is alive and he goes before us, summoning us to carry on the mission of nonviolence.

Our hearts burn with the fire of hope.

We have been changed forever. God has begun the revolution within us. We are sent out into the world as ambassadors of that revolutionary, nonviolent God. God sends us to prepare a new world for God right here on earth. Alive in faith, we take up the journey of nonviolent love.

Our prayer is constant: "Come, Lord Jesus."

ENDNOTES

chapter four
THE CALL

1. Ched Myers, *Binding the Strong Man* (Maryknoll: Orbis Books, 1988), 133.

chapter six
LOVE YOUR ENEMIES

1. King, Jr., Martin Luther. *Strength to Love* (Philadelphia: Fortress Press, 1981), 48.
2. Barclay, William. *The Gospel of Matthew* (Philadelphia: Westminster Press, 1958), 172–173.
3. King, Jr., Martin Luther. *Stride Toward Freedom* (New York: Harper and Row Publishers, 1958), 87–88.

chapter eight
THE NARROW GATE

1. Bill Wylie-Kellermann, ed. *A Keeper of the Word: Selected Writings of William Stringfellow* (Grand Rapids: Wm. Eerdmans Publishing Company, 1994), 69.

chapter ten
THE GOOD SHEPHERD

1. Judith Noone. *The Same Fate as the Poor* (Maryknoll: Orbis Books, 1995), 90.
2. Noone. 91–92.

chapter fourteen
WALKING ON WATER

1. Judith Noone, *The Same Fate as the Poor* (Maryknoll: Orbis Books, 1995), 115–116.

chapter fifteen
WHO DO YOU SAY THAT I AM?

1. Ched Myers, *Binding the Strong Man* (Maryknoll: Orbis Books, 1988), 247.

chapter nineteen
THE RICH YOUNG MAN

1. Ana Carrigan, *Salvador Witness: The Life and Calling of Jean Donovan* (New York: Simon and Schuster, 1984), 218.

chapter twenty-five
BROKEN BREAD, BLOOD SHED

1. James Brockman, *Romero: A Life* (Maryknoll: Orbis Books, 1989), 242.
2. Ibid., 244

chapter twenty-seven
JESUS' LAST WORDS: "PUT YOUR SWORD BACK!"

1. Ched Myers, *Binding the Strong Man* (Maryknoll: Orbis Books, 1987), 368.